1129
D

D1172067

KNITTING MASTERPIECES

*To Jane Belvedere of Sale, Cheshire,
and Madame Defarge:
'It is a far, far better thing that I knit . . .'*

KNITTING
MASTERPIECES

Ruth Herring and Karen Manners

Pantheon Books · New York

**Library of Congress
Cataloging-in-Publication Data**

Herring, Ruth.
   Knitting Masterpieces
   1. Sweaters. 2. Knitting – Patterns.
3. Art-Reproduction.
I. Manners, Karen. II. Title.
TT825.H47   1987   746.9'2 87-2233
ISBN 0-394-56266-6

Manufactured in Spain

CONTENTS

PREHISTORIC CAVE PAINTING
Standing Bison

The creators of these cave paintings, c. 1350 BC, believed that through the very act of portrayal, the strength of the animals depicted would be transferred to the hunters who gazed at them.

The bison has been interpreted with chunky yarn in earthy colors. Simple embroidered black lines represent the cracks in the cave walls.

SIZES
To fit 36 (38, 40, 42, 44)"/90 (95, 100, 105, 110) cm chest

MATERIALS
Anny Blatt No. 6
16 (17, 17, 18, 19) × 50g balls in Light Brown (shade 2275)
1 × 50g ball each in Black (shade 2272), Brown (shade 2276) and Rust (shade 2522)
A pair each of sizes 6 (4mm) and 7 (4½mm) knitting needles
One size 6 (4mm) circular knitting needle
One medium leather button
Stitch holder

GAUGE
16 sts. and 22 rows to 4"/10cm over St. st. worked on size 7 (4½mm) needles.
Check your gauge

Notes
Instructions for the larger sizes are given in parentheses ( ).

When working motif, use separate, small balls of yarn. When joining in a new color, leave an end of about 2½"/5cm for weaving in later, and when changing color, twist yarns together at back of work to avoid making a hole.

BACK
** Using smaller size needles and light brown yarn, cast on 84 (88, 92, 96, 100) sts.

Rib row 1: K. 1, p. 2, * k. 2, p. 2, rep. from * to last st., k. 1.

Rib row 2: P. 1, k. 2, * p. 2, k. 2, rep. from * to last st., p. 1.

Rep. these 2 rows for 2¾"/7cm, ending rib row 2, **

Change to larger size needles.

Proceeding in St. st., work 70 (72, 74, 78, 80) rows.

Shape armholes
Bind off 4 sts. at beg. of next 2 rows.
Continue in St. st. until 118 (124, 128, 134, 138) rows in St. st. is complete from beg., ending with a p. row.

Shape neck
Next row: K. 32 (34, 36, 38, 40) sts., turn and leave remaining sts. on a spare needle.
Work on these sts. for first side of neck.

Next row: Bind off 4 (4, 5, 6, 6) sts., p. to end.
K. 1 row.

Next row: Bind off 5 sts., p. to end.
Bind off.

Return to remaining sts.
With RS facing, slip first 12 sts. to a holder, join yarn to next st. and k. to end.
P. 1 row.

Next row: Bind off 4 (4, 5, 6, 6) sts., k. to end.
P. 1 row.

Next row: Bind off 5 sts., k. to end.
Bind off.

FRONT
Work as given for back from ** to **.
Change to larger size needles and work

in St. st. for 38 (40, 42, 46, 48) rows.

Place motif as follows:

Row 1: K. 53 (55, 57, 59, 61) light brown, 1 black, 2 light brown, 1 brown, 1 black, 26 (28, 30, 32, 34) light brown.

Row 2: P. 25 (27, 29, 31, 33) light brown, 2 black, 1 brown, 2 light brown, 2 black, 52 (54, 56, 58, 60) light brown.

Continue working from chart, shaping armholes on row 32 as for back, until row 59 has been completed.

Continuing in light brown only, work 1 (5, 7, 9, 11) rows St. st.

Shape neck

Next row: K. 38 (40, 42, 44, 46) sts., turn and leave remaining sts. on a spare needle.

Work on these sts. for first side of neck. Dec. 1 st. at neck edge on every row until 23 (25, 26, 27, 29) sts. remain. Work 8 (8, 7, 7, 6, 6) rows even.
Bind off.

Return to remaining sts.

With RS facing, rejoin yarn and k. to end. Work second side of neck to match first, reversing all shaping.

SLEEVES

Using smaller size needles and grège, cast on 36 (40, 42, 46, 50) sts.

Rib row 1: K. 1 (1, 2, 2, 2), * p. 2, k. 2, rep. from * to last 3 (3, 4, 4, 4) sts., p. 2, k. 1 (1, 2, 2, 2).

Rib row 2: P. 1 (1, 2, 2, 2), * k. 2, p. 2, rep. from * to last 3 (3, 4, 4, 4) sts., k. 2, p. 1 (1, 2, 2, 2).

Rep. these 2 rows for 2¾"/7cm, ending rib row 1.

Inc. row: Rib 7 (8, 9, 9, 10), M. 1, * rib 7 (8, 8, 9, 10), M. 1, rep. from * to last 8 (8, 9, 10, 10) sts., rib to end: 40 (44, 46, 50, 54) sts.

Change to larger size needles.
Proceed in St. st., increasing 1 st. each end of 5th row and then every 4th row until there are 76 (80, 84, 86, 90) sts. Work 15 (17, 15, 19, 21) rows even.
Bind off.

COLLAR

Join shoulder seams.

With RS facing, using circular needle and light brown, pick up and k. 24 (25, 26, 28, 28) sts. up right side of neck, 10 (11, 12, 12, 12) sts. down right back neck, k. across 12 sts. of center back neck, then pick up and k. 10 (11, 12, 12, 12) sts. up left side of back neck and 24 (25, 26, 28, 28) sts. down left front neck: 80 (84, 88, 92, 92) sts.

Working back and forth as with straight needles, p. 1 row.

Row 1: K. 1, p. 2, * k. 2, p. 2, rep. from * to last st., k. 1.

Row 2: P. 1, k. 2, * p. 2, k. 2, rep. from * to last st., p. 1.

Rep. these 2 rows 3 times more.

Next row: Rib to last 8 sts., bind off 4 sts., rib to end.

Next row: Rib 4, cast on 4 sts., rib to end. Rib 6 rows more.

Bind off in rib 10 sts. at beg. of next 2 rows, then bind off in rib 4 sts. at beg. of next 10 rows. Bind off in rib.

TO MAKE UP

Block and press pieces lightly under a damp cloth following instructions on ball band.

Sew in sleeves, then join side and sleeve seams. Sew on button to correspond with buttonhole at neck.

Work embroidery on Bison in black as indicated on chart.

Using black, embroider "cracks" in backstitch at intervals over the back and sleeves of sweater. Embroider the cracks also over shoulder and side seams, making them stand out boldly.

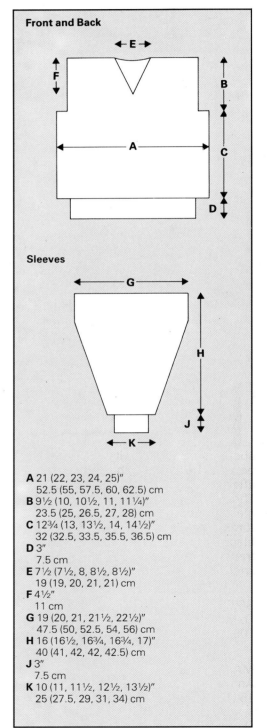

Front and Back

Sleeves

A 21 (22, 23, 24, 25)"
  52.5 (55, 57.5, 60, 62.5) cm
B 9½ (10, 10½, 11, 11¼)"
  23.5 (25, 26.5, 27, 28) cm
C 12¾ (13, 13½, 14, 14½)"
  32 (32.5, 33.5, 35.5, 36.5) cm
D 3"
  7.5 cm
E 7½ (7½, 8, 8½, 8½)"
  19 (19, 20, 21, 21) cm
F 4½"
  11 cm
G 19 (20, 21, 21½, 22½)"
  47.5 (50, 52.5, 54, 56) cm
H 16 (16½, 16¾, 16¾, 17)"
  40 (41, 42, 42, 42.5) cm
J 3"
  7.5 cm
K 10 (11, 11½, 12½, 13½)"
  25 (27.5, 29, 31, 34) cm

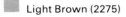 Light Brown (2275)

■ Black (2272)

■ Brown (2276)

■ Rust (2522)

⟋ Backstitch embroidery using Black (2272)

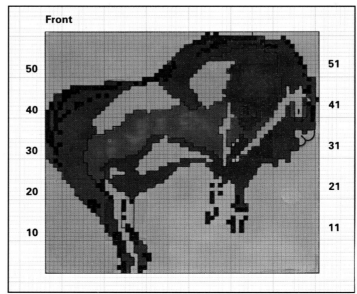

Front

50
40
30
20
10

51
41
31
21
11

EGYPTIAN
WALL PAINTING
The Pharaoh's Tomb

This period, c. 1500 BC, was called the Golden Age of Egyptian civilization. The complete painting shows Pharaoh Horemheb offering libations of wine and it is supposed to portray the glory of Pharaoh in the afterlife.

The sweater includes some of the hieroglyphics found in the Pharaoh's tomb. Their strong color and bold black lines make them easy to translate into jacquard and intarsia knitting.

SIZES
To fit 32 to 36 (38 to 42)"/80 to 90 (95 to 105) cm chest.

MATERIALS
Anny Blatt No. 4
15 (16) × 50g balls in Grey (shade 1295)
1 × 50g ball each in Black (shade 1310), Dark Green (shade 1881), Green (shade 2513), Orange (shade 2543), Écru (shade 1298) and Red (shade 1287)
A pair each of sizes 3 (3¼mm) and 6 (4mm) knitting needles
One size 3 (3¼mm) circular needle

GAUGE
22 sts. and 30 rows to 4"/10cm over St. st. worked on size 6 (4mm) needles.
Check your gauge

NOTES
Instructions for the larger sizes are given in parentheses ( ).
When working motif, use separate, small balls of yarn. When joining in a new color, leave an end of about 2"/5cm for weaving in later, and when changing color, twist yarns together at back of work to avoid making a hole.

BACK AND FRONT
(The same)
Using smaller size needles and sorrel, cast on 121 (131) sts.
Rib row 1: K. 1, * p. 1, k. 1, rep. from * to end.
Rib row 2: P. 1, * k. 1, p. 1, rep. from * to end.
Rep these 2 rows for 3"/7.5cm,

increasing 1 st. at beg. of last row: 122 (132) sts.
Change to larger size needles.
Beg. k. row, work 6 rows St. st.
Beg. row 7 of chart for back and front, work in pat. as follows:
Row 7: K. 37 (42) grey, 10 orange, 13 grey, 2 black, 4 grey, 10 dark green, 46 (51) grey.
Continue in pat. from chart until row 80 has been completed.
Work 2 (10) rows even in St. st.
Bind off.

SLEEVES AND YOKE
Using smaller size needles and sorrel, cast on 55 (61) sts.
Work in rib as given for back for 2½"/6.5cm, ending rib row 1.
Inc. row: Rib 3(7), M. 1, * rib 6, M. 1, rep. from * to last 4 (6) sts., rib to end: 64 (70) sts.
Change to larger size needles.
Working in St. st., work 2 rows grey and 2 rows écru.
1st size only
Change to grey and inc. 1 st. each end of next row.

Work 1 row.
2nd size only
Work 2 rows grey.
Next row: For 2nd size only increasing 1 st. each end of row, K. 2 orange, 1 black, **for both sizes** * k. 2 écru, 1 black, 4 dark green, 1 black, 2 écru, 1 black, 4 orange, 1 black, rep. from * to last 2 (5) sts., K. 2 écru, then **for 2nd size only** k. 1 black, 2 dark green.
Working in colors as established, work 3 rows **for 1st size only** increasing 1 st. each end of the 2nd row.
Work 2 rows in grey, then inc. 1 st. each end of next row, work 2 rows écru.
Continuing in grey only, inc. as before on every 4th (6th) row until there are 86 (96) sts.
Work 3 (5) rows even.
Increasing 1 st. each end of first row, work in pat. from chart for sleeves, increasing as indicated, until row 96 for right sleeve or row 97 for left sleeve has been completed.
Next row: Bind off 55 sts., work to end.
Continuing in grey only, work 29 rows even for right sleeve or 28 rows even for left sleeve.
Bind off.

TO MAKE UP
Block and press pieces lightly under a damp cloth following instructions on ball band. Join sleeves at center back. Matching center back seam to center of back, join back to back yoke. Join side and sleeve seams.

COLLAR
With RS facing, using circular needle and grey, pick up and k. 55 sts. up right side of front neck, 30 sts. across right back neck to center back seam, 29 sts. across left back neck and 55 sts. down left side of front neck: 169 sts.
Working back and forth as with straight needles, p. 1 row.
Work in rib as given for back for 8"/20cm. Bind off in rib.
Overlap right collar edge over left, then join front yoke to front.

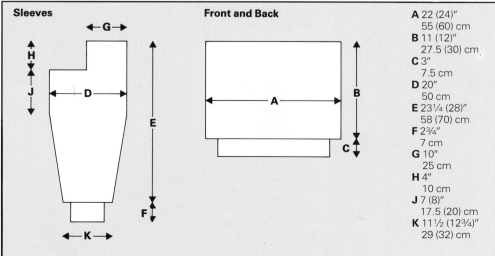

Sleeves

Front and Back

A 22 (24)"
55 (60) cm
B 11 (12)"
27.5 (30) cm
C 3"
7.5 cm
D 20"
50 cm
E 23¼ (28)"
58 (70) cm
F 2¾"
7 cm
G 10"
25 cm
H 4"
10 cm
J 7 (8)"
17.5 (20) cm
K 11½ (12¾)"
29 (32) cm

The Pharaoh's Tomb modeled by Janet Street Porter

EGYPTIAN WALL PAINTING

Grey (1295)

Black (1310)

Dark Green (1881)

Green (2513)

Orange (2543)

Écru (1298)

Red (1287)

Front and Back

80   81
70   71
60   61
50   51
40   41
30   31
20   21
10   11

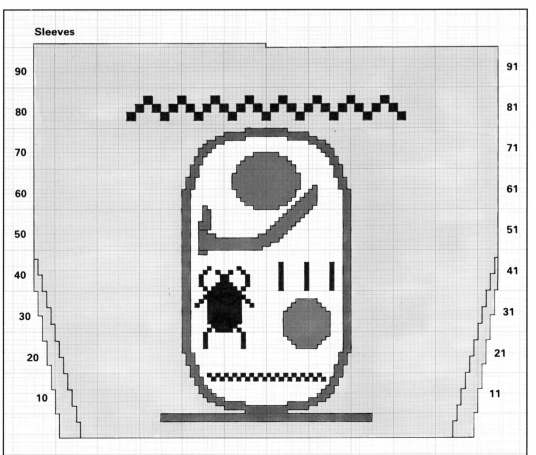

Sleeves

90   91
80   81
70   71
60   61
50   51
40   41
30   31
20   21
10   11

GRECIAN VASE: EXEKIAS
Achilles

This terracotta and black vase dating from c. 540 BC may be found in the British Museum, London. It is signed by the painter Exekias and is Athenian. It depicts Achilles slaying the Amazon Penthesilea.
The bands of patterns around the base and neck of the jar have been translated into jacquard knitting bordering the front panel of the sweater. The head and shoulders of Achilles are worked in intarsia.

SIZES
To fit 32 to 36 (38 to 42)"/80 to 90 (95 to 105) cm chest.

MATERIALS
Rowan Yarns Lightweight D.K.
15 (17) × 25g balls in Terra Cotta (shade 620)
11 × 50g balls in Black (shade 62)
4 × 50g balls in Rust (shade 27)
2 × 50g balls in Écru (shade 1)
A pair each of sizes 3 (3¼mm) and 6 (4mm) knitting needles

One size 3 (3¼mm) circular needle
Stitch holder

GAUGE
22 sts. and 27 rows to 4"/10cm over St. st. worked on size 6 (4mm) needles.
Check your gauge

NOTES
Instructions for the larger sizes are given in parentheses ( ).
When working motif, use separate, small balls of yarn. When joining in a new color, leave an end of about 2"/5cm for weaving in later, and when changing color, twist yarns together at back of work to avoid making a hole.

BACK
** Using smaller size needles and black, cast on 122 (132) sts.
Rib row 1: K. 1, * p. 1, k. 1, rep. from * to end.
Rib row 2: P. 1, * k. 1, p. 1, rep. from * to end.
Rep. these 2 rows for 3"/7.5cm.
Continuing in rib, bind off 28 (33) sts. at beg. of next 2 rows: 66 sts. **

Change to larger size needles.
Break off black. Join in terra cotta.
Beg. k. row, work 144 (158) rows in St. st.
Shape back neck
Next row: K. 18, turn and leave remaining sts. on a spare needle.
Bind off 9 sts. at beg. of next row.
Work 1 row. Bind off.
Return to remaining sts.
With RS facing, slip first 30 sts. to a holder, join yarn to next st. and k. to end.
P. 1 row.
Bind off 9 sts. at beg. of next row.
Work 1 row. Bind off.

FRONT
Work as given for back from ** to **.
Change to larger size needles.
Beg. at row 9 (1), work in pat. from chart until row 102 has been completed.
Bind off.

SLEEVES
Using smaller size needles and black, cast on 53 (59) sts.
Rib row 1: K. 1, * p. 1, k. 1, rep. from * to end.

EXEKIAS

Rib row 2: P. 1, * k. 1, p. 1, rep. from * to end.
Rep. these 2 rows for 2¾"/7cm, ending rib row 1.
Inc. row: Rib 5, M. 1, * rib 6 (7), M. 1, rep. from * to last 6 (5) sts., rib to end: 61 (67) sts.
Change to larger size needles.
Working from chart for cuff, place pat. as follows:
Row 1: K. 2 (5) black, 1 terra cotta, * 7

black, 1 terra cotta, rep. from * to last 2 (5) sts., k. 2 (5) black.
Inc. 1 st. each end of row 5 and row 9, continue in pat. until row 10 has been completed.
Continuing in terra cotta only, inc. 1 st. each end of 3rd row and every following 4th row until there are 93 (99) sts., ending p. row.
Now inc. 1 st. each end of next row and then every other row to 113 (121) sts.,

Terra Cotta (620)

Black (62)

Rust (27)

Écru (1)

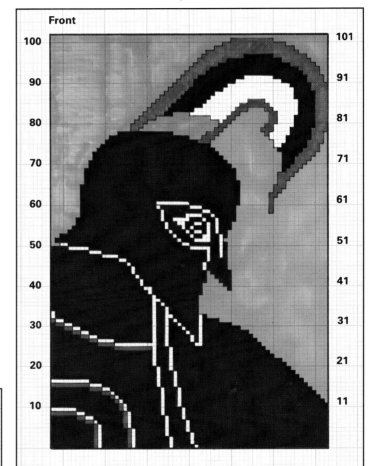

Front

100   101
90   91
80   81
70   71
60   61
50   51
40   41
30   31
20   21
10   11

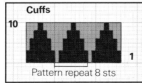

Cuffs

10

1

Pattern repeat 8 sts

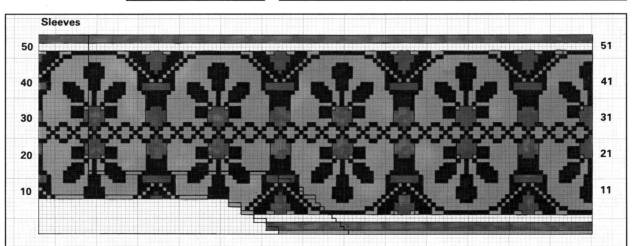

Sleeves

50   51
40   41
30   31
20   21
10   11

EXEKIAS

then each end of every row until there are 115 (133) sts.

2nd size only
Cast on 3 sts. at beg. of next 5 rows; 148 sts.

Both sizes
Next row: Beg. at row 1 of chart for sleeve.

For 1st size inc. 1 st. each end of row.
For 2nd size cast on 3 sts. at beg. of row.

Work in pat. and inc. where indicated until row 50 has been completed: 243 (267) sts.
Bind off.

TO MAKE UP
Block and press pieces lightly under a damp cloth following instructions on ball band. Sew in sleeves, sewing in front and back panels and stretching ribs to fit row ends of side panels. Join side and sleeve seams.

COLLAR
With RS facing, using circular needle and black, pick up and k. 44 (50) sts. up right side of front neck, 19 sts. down right side of back neck, k. across 30 sts. from holder, pick up and k. 20 sts. up right side of back neck then 44 (50) sts. down left side of front neck: 157 (169) sts.
Working back and forth as with straight needles, p. 1 row.
Work 6"/15cm in rib as given for back. Bind off in rib.
Stitch row-ends of collar into place at top of front panel, then join bound-off edges of collar for approximately 2"/5cm.

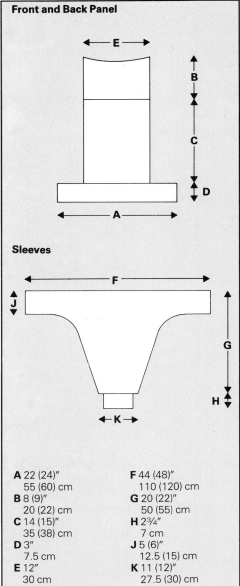

Front and Back Panel

Sleeves

A 22 (24)"
  55 (60) cm
B 8 (9)"
  20 (22) cm
C 14 (15)"
  35 (38) cm
D 3"
  7.5 cm
E 12"
  30 cm

F 44 (48)"
  110 (120) cm
G 20 (22)"
  50 (55) cm
H 2¾"
  7 cm
J 5 (6)"
  12.5 (15) cm
K 11 (12)"
  27.5 (30) cm

IMPERIAL COINAGE

Roman Emperor

The head is probably Julius Caesar, taken from a Roman coin *c.* 55 BC. This style of portraiture on coins, with laurel wreaths and ribbons adorning the head of the monarch, was popular throughout Europe until the beginning of this century.
The classical frieze makes a strong border design for this sweater.

SIZES
To fit 32 (34, 36, 38)"/80 (85, 90, 95) cm chest.

MATERIALS
Scheepjeswool Superwash Zermatt
8 (9, 10, 10) × 50g balls Cream (shade 4812)
11 (11, 12, 12) × 50g balls Charcoal (shade 4864)
1 × 50g ball Grey (shade 4806)
A pair each of sizes 3 (3¼mm) and 6 (4mm) knitting needles

GAUGE
22 sts. and 30 rows to 4"/10cm over St. st. worked on size 6 (4mm) needles.

Check your gauge

NOTES
Instructions for the larger sizes are given in parentheses ( ).
When working motif, use separate, small balls of yarn. When joining in a new color, leave an end of about 2"/5cm for weaving in later, and when changing color, twist yarns together at back of work to avoid making a hole.

BACK
** Using smaller size needles and charcoal, cast on 107 (113, 117, 123) sts.
Rib row 1: K. 1, * p. 1, k. 1, rep. from * to end.
Rib row 2: P. 1, * k. 1, p. 1, rep. from * to end.
Rep. these 2 rows for 3½"/9cm, ending rib row 1.
Inc. row: Rib 6 (8, 10, 14), M. 1, * rib 12, M. 1, rep. from * to last 5 (9, 11, 13) sts., rib to end: 116 (122, 126, 132) sts. **
Change to larger size needles.
Work in pat. from chart, working armhole shaping as indicated, until row 172 (174, 176, 180) has been completed.
Shape neck
Next row: Continuing in pat. following chart, k. 38 (39, 41, 43), turn and leave remaining sts. on a spare needle.
Work on these sts. only.
Next row: Bind off 5 sts., p. to end.
K. 1 row.
Next row: Bind off 5 sts., p. to end.
Bind off.
Return to remaining sts.
With RS facing, rejoin yarn and bind off first 18 (22, 22, 24) sts., then k. to end.
P. 1 row.
Next row: Bind off 5 sts., k. to end.
P. 1 row.
Next row: Bind off 5 sts., k. to end.
Bind off.

FRONT
Work as given for back from ** to **.
Change to larger size needles.
Work in pat. from chart, shaping armholes as indicated, until row 158 (160, 162, 166) has been completed.
Shape neck
Next row: K. 37 (40, 42, 45), turn and

leave remaining sts. on a spare needle.
Work on these sts. only.
Dec. 1 st. at neck edge on every row
until 28 (29, 31, 33) sts. remain.
Work 8 (6, 6, 5) rows even.
Bind off.
Return to remaining sts.
With RS facing, rejoin yarn and bind off
first 20 sts., k. to end.

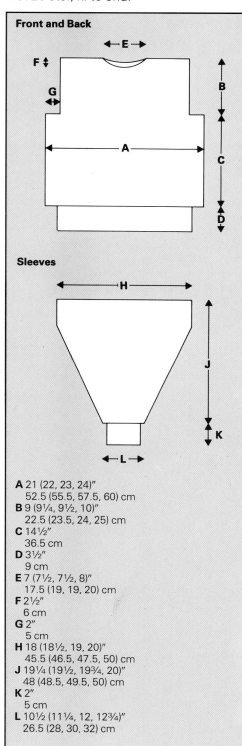

Front and Back

Sleeves

A 21 (22, 23, 24)"
  52.5 (55.5, 57.5, 60) cm
B 9 (9¼, 9½, 10)"
  22.5 (23.5, 24, 25) cm
C 14½"
  36.5 cm
D 3½"
  9 cm
E 7 (7½, 7½, 8)"
  17.5 (19, 19, 20) cm
F 2½"
  6 cm
G 2"
  5 cm
H 18 (18½, 19, 20)"
  45.5 (46.5, 47.5, 50) cm
J 19¼ (19½, 19¾, 20)"
  48 (48.5, 49.5, 50) cm
K 2"
  5 cm
L 10½ (11¼, 12, 12¾)"
  26.5 (28, 30, 32) cm

Now complete to match first side of
neck, reversing all shaping.

SLEEVES

Using smaller size needles and charcoal,
cast on 53 (57, 61, 65) sts.
Rep. the 2 rib rows as given for back for
2"/5cm, ending rib row 1.
Inc. row: Rib 10, M. 1, * rib 8 (9, 10, 11),
M. 1, rep. from * to last 11 sts., rib to
end: 58 (62, 66, 70) sts.
Change to larger size needles.
Using charcoal, work 3 rows St. st.
Now beg. at row 6 of chart, work in pat.
as follows:
Next row: For 4th size only p. 1
charcoal, **for all sizes** p. 9 (11, 13, 14)
cream, * p. 2 charcoal, p. 14 cream, rep.
from * to last 1 (3, 5, 7) sts., p. 1 (2, 2, 2)
charcoal, then **for (2nd, 3rd and 4th)
sizes only** p. (1, 3, 5) cream.
Beg. at row 7, continue working from
chart until row 24 has been completed,
then continue in charcoal only and *at the
same time* inc. 1 st. each end of row 7
and then every 4th row until there are
100 (102, 104, 110) sts.
Work 3 (7, 11, 7) rows even.
Now work rows 1 to 4 of chart.
Beg. row 5 from chart, work in pat. as
follows:
Next row: For 1st and 4th sizes only

p. 14 (3) cream, **for all sizes** p. 2 (1, 2, 2)
charcoal, * p. 14 cream, p. 2 charcoal,
rep. from * to last 4 (5, 6, 9) sts., p. 4 (5,
6, 9) cream.
Continue in pat. as set until row 24 has
been completed.
Change to charcoal and work 32 (34, 36,
38) rows even.
Bind off.

COLLAR

With WS together, join left shoulder
seam.
With RS facing, using smaller size
needles and charcoal, pick up and k. 49
(53, 53, 55) sts. across back neck, 32 (33,
34, 35) sts. down left front neck, 20 sts.
across front neck and 32 (33, 34, 35) sts.
up right front neck: 133 (139, 141, 145)
sts.
P. 1 row.
Work 3½"/9cm in rib as given for back.
Bind off in rib.

TO MAKE UP

Block and press pieces lightly under a
damp cloth following band instructions.
With WS together, join right shoulder
and collar seams.
Joining bound-off edge of armhole to
underarms, sew in sleeves, then join
side and sleeve seams.

Roman Emperor
modeled by Susan
George

IMPERIAL COINAGE

Cream (4812)

Charcoal (4864)

Grey (4806)

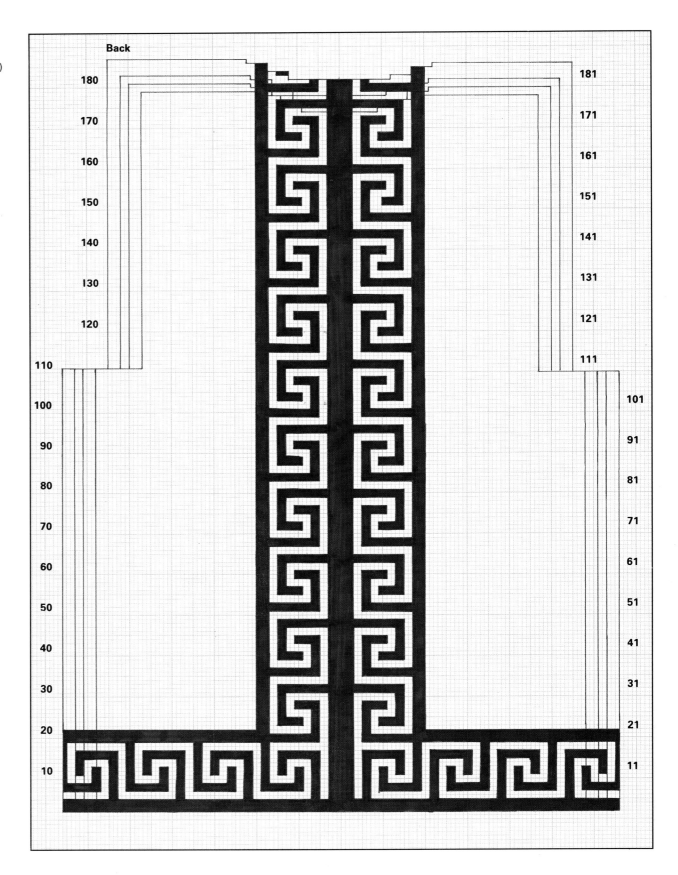

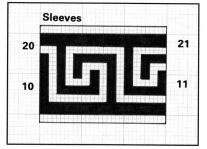

Sleeves

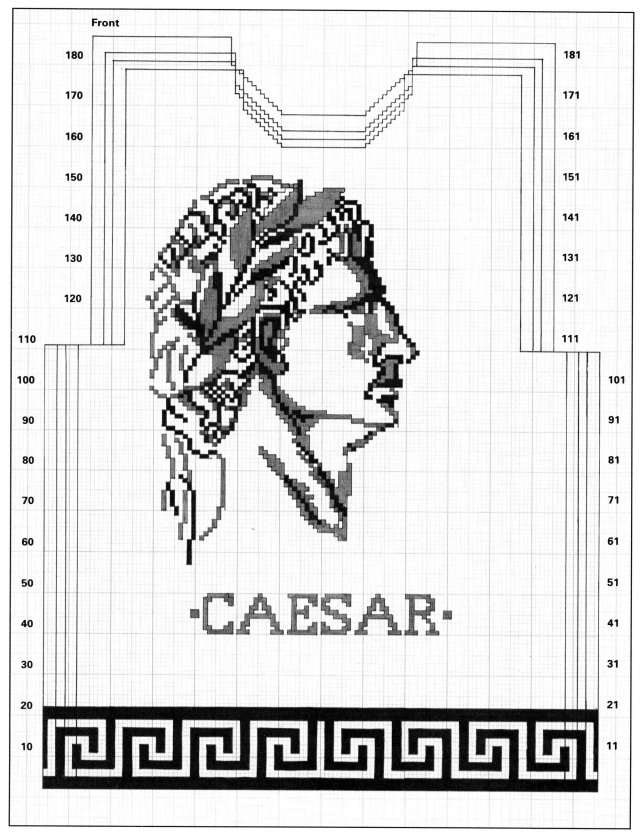

Front

·CAESAR·

BAYEUX TAPESTRY

Halley's Comet

Although called a tapestry, it was in fact worked in embroidery stitches and not woven on a loom and is one of the earliest, and certainly the greatest, strip cartoons, dating from around AD 1070–1080. It depicts the Norman conquest of England. The artist or artists are unknown, but the embroidery was almost certainly worked in England, possibly by the School of Embroidery at Canterbury, Kent. It was commissioned by Bishop Odo to be hung in his cathedral at Bayeux.

The scene depicted on the sweater shows Halley's Comet which would have been clearly visible in the sky in February 1066. It has been worked all around the sweater, including the raglan sleeves. The hand and facial details have been worked in embroidery.

SIZES
One size only to fit 38 to 44"/95 to 110cm chest

MATERIALS
Brunswick Germantown
6 × 100g balls of White (shade 400)
1 × 100g ball each of Jute Heather (shade 439), Burgundy (shade 422), Black (shade 460) and Teal (shade 4033)
A pair each of sizes 6 (4mm) and 8 (5mm) knitting needles
Stitch holders

GAUGE
19 sts. and 24 rows to 4"/10cm over St. st. worked on size 8 (5mm) needles.
Check your gauge

NOTES
When working motif, use separate, small balls of yarn. When joining in a new color, leave an end of about 2"/5cm for weaving in later, and when changing color, twist yarns together at back of work to avoid making a hole.

BACK
** With smaller size needles and white, cast on 107 sts.
Rib row 1: K. 1, * p. 1, k. 1, rep. from * to end.

Halley's Comet
modeled by John
Gordon Sinclair

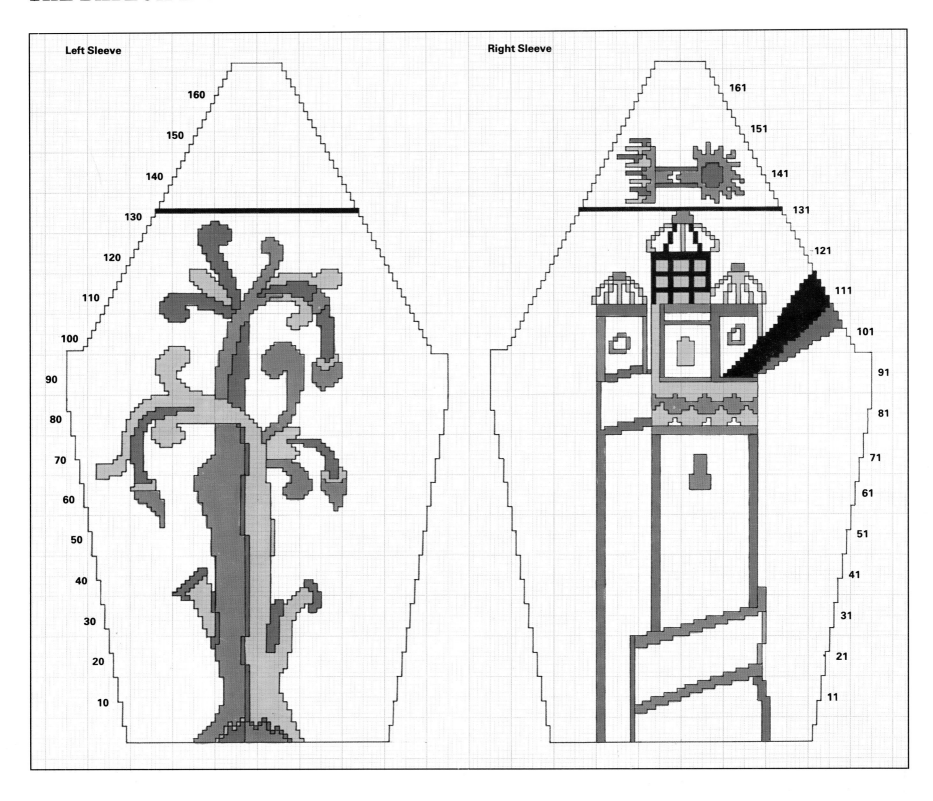

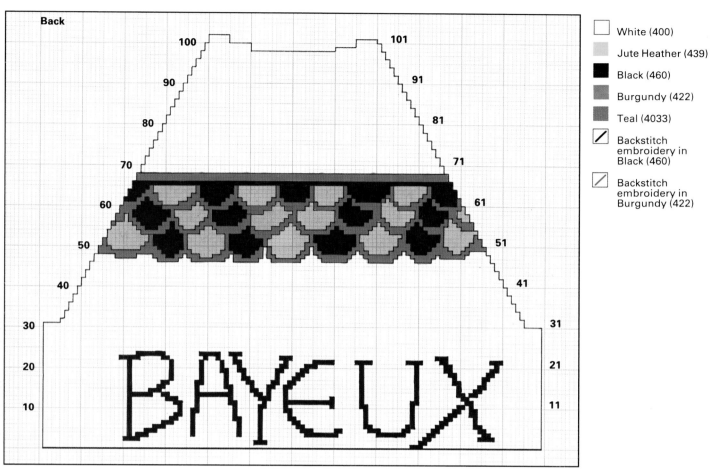

Back

100   101
90   91
80   81
70   71
60   61
50   51
40   41
30   31
20   21
10   11

BAYEUX

White (400)

Jute Heather (439)

Black (460)

Burgundy (422)

Teal (4033)

Backstitch embroidery in Black (460)

Backstitch embroidery in Burgundy (422)

THE BAYEUX TAPESTRY

Rib row 2: P. 1, * k. 1, p. 1, rep. from * to end.
Rep. these 2 rows for 3"/7.5cm, ending rib row 1.
Inc. row: Rib 8, * M. 1, rib 9, rep. from * to end: 118 sts. **
Change to larger size needles.
Work 48 rows St. st.
Working in pat. from chart for back, continue as follows:
Row 1: K. 28 white, 3 black, 87 white.
Row 2: P. 50 white, join in a 2nd ball of black and p. 3 black, 36 white, 2 black, 27 white.
Continue in pat. from chart until row 30

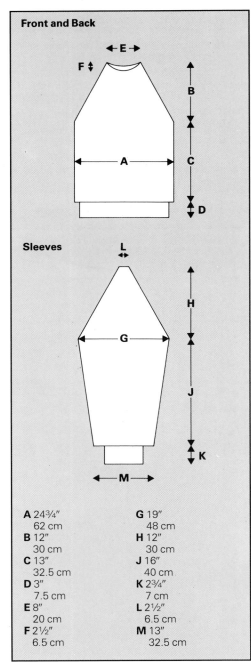

Front and Back

E
F
B
A
C
D

Sleeves

L
H
G
J
K
M

A 24¾"		**G** 19"	
62 cm		48 cm	
B 12"		**H** 12"	
30 cm		30 cm	
C 13"		**J** 16"	
32.5 cm		40 cm	
D 3"		**K** 2¾"	
7.5 cm		7 cm	
E 8"		**L** 2½"	
20 cm		6.5 cm	
F 2½"		**M** 13"	
6.5 cm		32.5 cm	

has been completed.
Shape raglans
Bind off 4 sts. at beg. of next 2 rows.
Dec. 1 st. at each end of the next row and then every other row until 96 sts. remain.
P. 1 row.
Continuing to dec. as before and beg. at row 47, work in pat. from chart until row 68 has been completed.
Continue in white only, dec. 1 st. at each end of the next row and then every other row until 44 sts. remain, ending with a p. row.
Shape back neck
Next row: K. 2 tog., k. 10, turn and leave remaining sts. on a spare needle.
Next row: Bind off 5 sts., p. to end.
Next row: K. 2 tog., k. to end: 5 sts. Bind off.
Return to remaining sts.
With RS facing, slip first 20 sts. to a holder, join yarn to next st. and k. to last 2 sts., k. 2 tog.
P. 1 row.
Next row: Bind off 5 sts., k. to last 2 sts., k. 2 tog.
P. 1 row, then bind off remaining 5 sts.

FRONT
Work as given for back from ** to **
Change to larger size needles.
Work in pat. from chart for front as follows:
Row 1: K. 5 white, 10 jute heather, 12 white, 6 black, 15 jute heather, 4 teal, 12 jute heather, 1 white, 1 jute heather, 9 white, 18 black, 25 white.
Row 2: P. 26 white, 16 black, 11 white, 2 jute heather, 2 white, 6 jute heather, 9 teal, 13 jute heather, 6 black, 12 white, 9 jute heather, 1 teal, 5 white.
Continue in pat. from chart, shaping raglan as given for back until row 138 has been completed: 52 sts.
Shape neck
Next row: Continuing in white only, k. 2 tog., k. 14, turn and leave remaining sts. on a spare needle.
Decreasing at raglan edge as before, dec. 1 st. at neck edge every row until 2 sts. remain.
Next row: K. 2 tog. and fasten off.
Return to remaining sts.
With RS facing, slip first 20 sts. to a holder, join on yarn and complete to match first side of neck, reversing all shaping.

LEFT SLEEVE
Using smaller size needles and white, cast on 51 sts.

Work in rib as given for back for 2¾"/7cm, ending rib row 1.
Inc. row: Rib 5, M. 1, * rib 4, M. 1, rep. from * to last 6 sts., rib to end: 62 sts.
Change to larger size needles.
Work in pat. from chart for left sleeve as follows:
Row 1: K. 20 white, 3 jute heather, 1 burgundy, 10 teal, 6 burgundy, 1 jute heather, 5 teal, 16 white.
Row 2: P. 17 white, 5 teal, 1 jute heather, 5 burgundy, 9 teal, 1 burgundy, 3 jute heather, 21 white.
Continue in pat. from chart and *at the same time* inc. 1 st. each end of the 5th row and then every 6th row until there are 90 sts.
Work even in pat. until row 96 has been completed.
Keeping pat. correct, shape raglan as given for back until 12 sts. remain, ending p. row.
Break off yarn and leave sts. on a holder.

RIGHT SLEEVE
Work cuff as given for left sleeve until the increase row is completed: 62 sts.
Work in pat. from chart for right sleeve as follows:
Row 1: K. 10 white, 2 burgundy, 30 white, 1 burgundy, 6 white, 2 burgundy, 11 white.
Row 2: P. 11 white, 2 burgundy, 6 white, 1 burgundy, 30 white, 2 burgundy, 10 white.
Continuing in pat. from chart for right sleeve, complete as given for left sleeve.

NECKBAND
Join front and left back raglan seams.
With RS facing and using smaller size needles and white, pick up and k. 10 sts. down right side of back neck, k. across 20 sts. on holder, pick up and k. 11 sts. up left side of back neck, k. across 12 sts. at top of left sleeve, pick up and k. 12 sts. down left side of front neck, k. across 20 sts. on holder, pick up and k. 12 sts. up right side of front neck, then k. across 12 sts. of right sleeve: 109 sts.
P. 1 row.
Work 8 rows in rib as given for back.
Bind off in rib.

TO MAKE UP
Block and press pieces lightly under a damp cloth following band instructions.
Join right back raglan and neckband seam.
Join side and sleeve seams. Using backstitch, embroider face, hand and spear as indicated on chart.

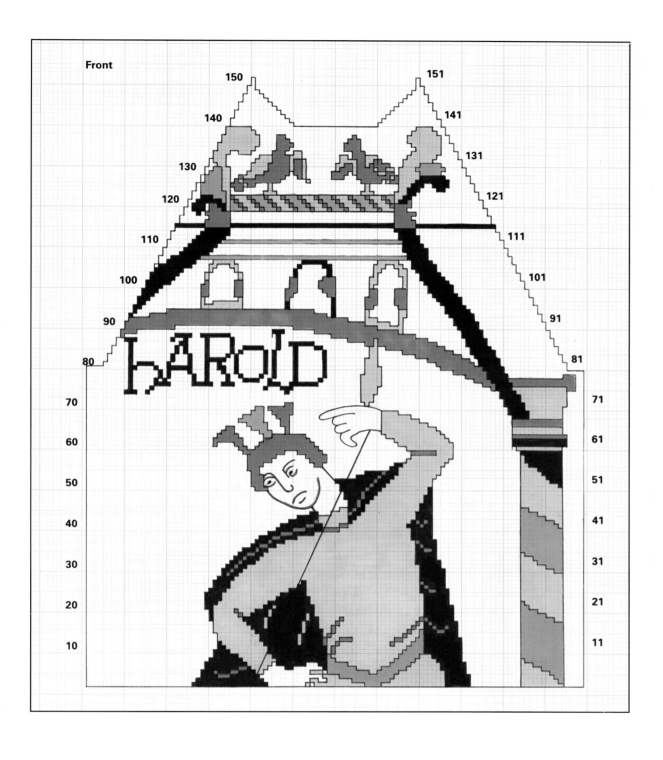

MICHELANGELO

Head of David

"David with the sling And I with the bow,"–Michelangelo. These were the words written on the first sketch for the statue, which was completed on 25 January 1504. It is probably the most famous sculpture of all time, worked from a flawed piece of marble originally offered to Leonardo da Vinci. Here, marble-effect colors have been chosen in pure wool to create an impression of the head of David in intarsia knitting.

SIZES
One size only to fit 32 to 38"/80 to 95cm chest

MATERIALS
Pingouin 4 Pingouins 100% Pure New Wool
10 × 50g balls of Écru (shade 08)
1 × 50g ball each of Sable (shade 19) and Camel (shade 18)
A pair each of sizes 2 (3mm) and 5 (3¾mm) knitting needles
Stitch holders

GAUGE
23 sts. and 31 rows to 4"/10cm over St. st. worked on size 5 (3¾mm) needles.
Check your gauge

NOTES
When working motif, use separate, small balls of yarn. When joining in a new color, leave an end of about 2"/5cm for weaving in later, and when changing color, twist yarns together at back of work to avoid making a hole.

BACK
** Using smaller size needles and écru, cast on 131 sts.
Rib row 1: K. 1, * p. 1, k. 1, rep. from * to end.
Rib row 2: P. 1, * k. 1, p. 1, rep. from * to end.
Rep. these 2 rows for 3"/7.5cm increasing 1 st. at end of last row: 132 sts. **
Change to larger size needles.
Beg. k. row, work 100 rows St. st.
Shape armholes
Bind off 6 sts. at beg. of next 2 rows.
Continue without shaping until 174 rows

St. st. altogether have been completed.
Shape back neck
Next row: K. 50, turn and leave remaining sts. on a spare needle.
Next row: Bind off 7 sts., p. to end.
K. 1 row.
Next row: Bind off 6 sts., p. to end.
Bind off.
Return to remaining sts.
With RS facing, slip first 20 sts. to a holder, join on yarn and k. to end.
P. 1 row.
Next row: Bind off 7 sts., k. to end.
P. 1 row.
Next row: Bind off 6 sts., k. to end.
Bind off.

FRONT
Work as given for back from ** to **.
Change to larger size needles.
Work in pat. as given on chart for front until row 154 has been completed.
Shape front neck
Next row: K. 50, turn and leave remaining sts. on a spare needle.
Dec. 1 st. at neck edge on every row until 37 sts. remain.
Work 10 rows even.

MICHELANGELO

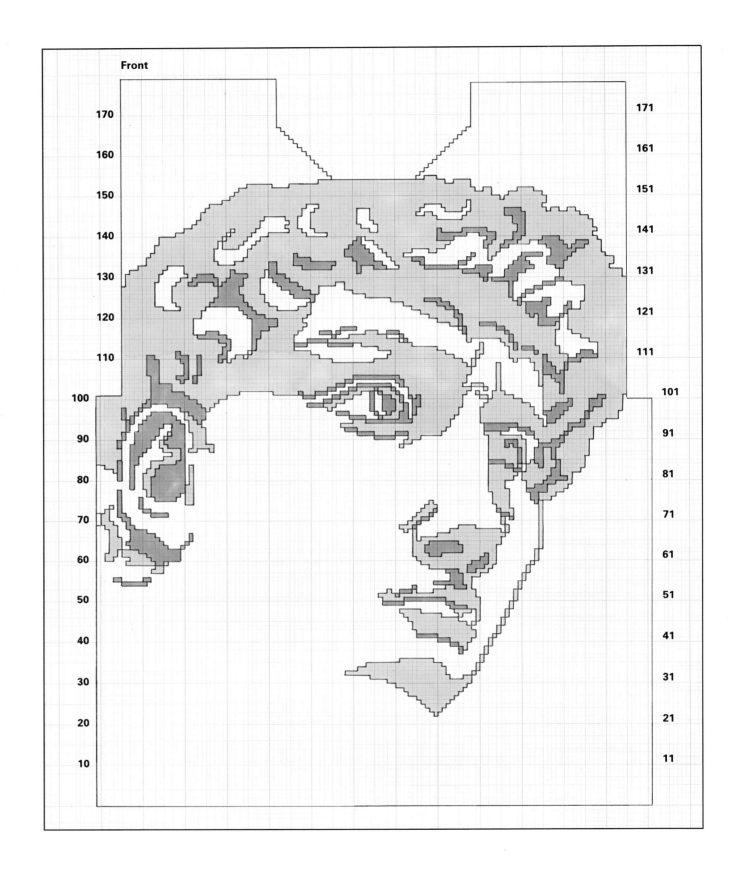

Sleeves

20 | 21
10 | 11

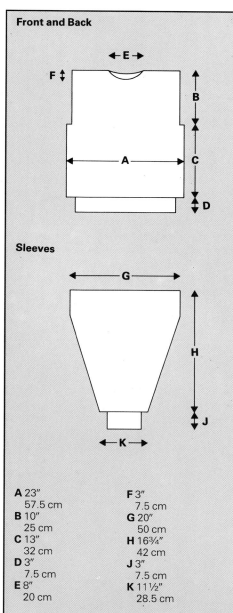

Front and Back

E
F ↕
B
A | C
D

Sleeves

G
H
J
K

A 23"
  57.5 cm
B 10"
  25 cm
C 13"
  32 cm
D 3"
  7.5 cm
E 8"
  20 cm

F 3"
  7.5 cm
G 20"
  50 cm
H 16¾"
  42 cm
J 3"
  7.5 cm
K 11½"
  28.5 cm

Bind off.
Return to remaining sts.
With RS facing, slip first 20 sts. to a
holder, join on yarn and k. to end.
Now complete 2nd side of neck to match
first, reversing all shaping.

SLEEVES
Using smaller size needles and écru, cast
on 63 sts.
Work 3"/7.5cm in rib as given for back,
ending rib row 1.
Inc. row: * Rib 16, M. 1, rep. from *
twice more, rib to end: 66 sts.
Change to larger size needles.
Work in St. st. increasing 1 st. each end
of 5th row and then every 4th row until
there are 116 sts.
Work 9 rows even, so ending with a p.
row.
Now work in pat. from chart for sleeve
until row 20 has been completed.
Bind off.

NECKBAND
Join left shoulder seam.
With RS facing and using smaller size
needles and écru, pick up and k. 17 sts.
up right side of back neck, k. across 20
sts. from back neck holder, pick up and k.
18 sts. up left side of back neck and 25
sts. down left side of front neck, k.
across 20 sts. from front neck holder,
then pick up and k. 25 sts. up right side
of front neck: 125 sts.
P. 1. row, then work 8 rows in rib as
given for back.
Bind off in rib.

TO MAKE UP
Block and press pieces lightly under a
damp cloth following instructions on ball
band.
Join right shoulder and neckband seam.
Fold neckband in half to wrong side and
slipstitch into position. Sew in sleeves.
Join side and sleeve seams.

LEONARDO
DA VINCI

Mona Lisa

Leonardo painted this picture from 1503–1505 and kept it by him until his death. The enigmatic smile and the haunting rocky landscape give this work a sense of mystery. He has created an almost androgynous human being from what started out as a simple portrait of a Florentine lady. That famous face has been reconstructed in knitting using subtle hues. The pattern was drawn with "half-closed eyes" and shows how the relief of the features can be achieved with simple areas of color.

SIZES
To fit 32 (34, 36, 38)"/80 (85, 90, 95) cm chest

MATERIALS
Anny Blatt No. 4
9 (9, 10, 10) × 50g balls in Olive (shade 1307)
1 × 50g ball each in Black (shade 1310), Beige (shade 1299), Oatmeal (shade 1301), Brown (shade 1303), Green (shade 2513) and Camel (shade 1300)

A pair each of sizes 3 (3¼mm) and 6 (4mm) knitting needles

GAUGE
22 sts. and 30 rows to 4"/10cm over St. st. worked on size 6 (4mm) needles.
Check your gauge

NOTES
Instructions for the larger sizes are given in parentheses ( ).
When working motif, use separate, small balls of yarn. When joining in a new color, leave an end of about 2"/5cm for weaving in later, and when changing color, twist yarns together at back of work to avoid making a hole.

BACK
** Using smaller size needles and olive, cast on 113 (117, 123, 129) sts.
Rib row 1: K. 1, * p. 1, k. 1, rep. from * to end.
Rib row 2: P. 1, * k. 1, p. 1, rep. from * to end.
Rep. these 2 rows for 2¼"/6cm, inc. 1 st. at end of last row: 114 (118, 124, 130) sts. **

Mona Lisa
modeled by
Michelle Collins

Change to larger needles.
Proceeding in St. st., work 72 rows.

Shape armholes

Bind off 6 sts. at beg. of next 2 rows: 102 (106, 112, 118) sts.

Continue even in St. st. until 74 (74, 76, 76) rows have been worked from beg. of armhole shaping.

Shape back neck

Next row: K. 30 (32, 35, 38), turn and leave remaining sts. on a spare needle. Work on these sts. only for first side.

Next row: Bind off 4 sts., p. to end.

Bind off.

Return to remaining sts.

With RS facing, join on yarn and bind off first 42 sts., k. to end.

P. 1 row.

Next row: Bind off 4 sts., k. to end.

Bind off.

FRONT

Work as given for back from ** to **.

Change to larger needles.

Work 2 rows in St. st.

Place motif as follows:

Row 1: K. 26 (28, 31, 34) black, 7 camel, 3 black, 1 green, 4 black, 2 green, 8 black, 4 green, 2 beige, 7 green, 1 beige, 2 green, 16 black, 1 camel, 2 green, 9 camel, 10 black, 9 (11, 14, 17) green.

Row 2: P. 10 (12, 15, 18) green, 13 black, 3 camel, 1 black, 3 green, 1 camel,

16 black, 2 green, 1 beige, 7 green, 3 beige, 3 green, 8 black, 3 green, 3 black, 2 green, 3 black, 8 camel, 24 (26, 29, 32) black.

Continue working from chart, shaping armholes as indicated, until row 115 has been completed.

Using olive only, work 13 (13, 15, 15) rows even.

Shape neck

Next row: K. 38 (40, 43, 46), turn and leave remaining sts. on a spare needle. Work on these sts. only for first side of neck.

Dec. 1 st. at neck edge on every row until 26 (28, 31, 34) sts. remain.

Work 5 (5, 7, 7) rows even.

Bind off.

Return to remaining sts.

With RS facing, join on yarn and bind off the first 26 sts., k. to end.

Now complete second side of neck to match first, reversing all shaping.

SLEEVES

Using smaller size needles and olive, cast on 59 (59, 61, 63) sts.

Work in rib as given for back for 2¼"/6cm, ending rib row 1.

Inc. row: Rib 8 (8, 10, 10), M. 1, * rib 7, M. 1, rep. from * to last 9 (9, 9, 11) sts., rib to end: 66 (66, 68, 70) sts.

Change to larger needles.

Proceed in St. st., increasing 1 st. each end of 5th row and then every 4th row until there are 110 (110, 116, 116) sts.

Work 15 (19, 15, 19) rows even.

Bind off.

COLLAR

Using smaller needles and olive, cast on 143 (143, 147, 147) sts.

Row 1: K. 1, * p. 1, k. 1, rep. from * to end.

Row 2: P. 1, * k. 1, p. 1, rep. from * to end.

Row 3: K. 1, p. 1, k. 3 tog. tbl., rib to last 5 sts., k. 3 tog., p. 1, k. 1.

Row 4: As row 2.

Rep. rows 3 and 4 until 111 (111, 115, 115) sts. remain.

Rep. row 2 once, then rows 1 and 2 once more.

Bind off loosely in rib.

TO MAKE UP

Block and press pieces lightly under a damp cloth following band instructions.

Join shoulder seams. With WS together, stitch bound-off edge of collar to neck edge.

Join edges of collar at center front for ¾"/2cm.

Sew in the sleeves, then join side and sleeve seams.

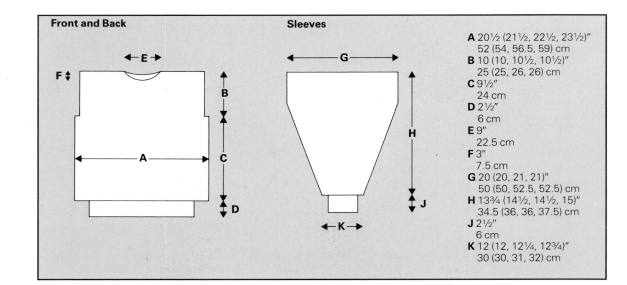

Front and Back   **Sleeves**

A 20½ (21½, 22½, 23½)"
52 (54, 56.5, 59) cm
B 10 (10, 10½, 10½)"
25 (25, 26, 26) cm
C 9½"
24 cm
D 2½"
6 cm
E 9"
22.5 cm
F 3"
7.5 cm
G 20 (20, 21, 21)"
50 (50, 52.5, 52.5) cm
H 13¾ (14½, 14½, 15)"
34.5 (36, 36, 37.5) cm
J 2½"
6 cm
K 12 (12, 12¼, 12¾)"
30 (30, 31, 32) cm

Olive (1307)

Black (1310)

Beige (1299)

Oatmeal (1301)

Brown (1303)

Green (2513)

Camel (1300)

RAPHAEL
Cherubs

The *Sistine Madonna*, from which these cherubs were taken, was painted between 1513 and 1516 and epitomizes the theatrical feel of much of Raphael's work. The picture displays a rare degree of tenderness and incorporates humorous details such as the bemused cherubs, which are among the most charming characters to be found in Renaissance painting. The cherubs have been knitted in chunky wool to give them a ''chubby'' look and the pale grey, white and camel dyes of this pure fiber give a subtle effect to the overall design.

SIZES
One size only to fit 32 to 38"/80 to 95cm chest

MATERIALS
Patons Beehive Shetland Chunky
10 × 50g balls in Grey (shade 2128)
2 × 50g balls in White (shade 2110)
1 × 50g ball each in Natural (shade 2102), Camel (shade 2103), Écru (shade 2101) and Brown (shade 2105)

A pair each of sizes 8 (5mm) and 10 (6mm) knitting needles
Stitch holders

GAUGE
15 sts. and 19 rows to 4"/10cm over St. st. worked on size 10 (6mm) needles.
Check your gauge

NOTES
When working motif, use separate, small balls of yarn. When joining in a new color, leave an end of about 2"/5cm for weaving in later, and when changing color, twist yarns together at back of work to avoid making a hole.

BACK
** Using smaller size needles and grey, cast on 95 sts.
Rib row 1: K. 1, * p. 1, k. 1, rep. from * to end.
Rib row 2: P. 1, * k. 1, p. 1, rep. from * to end.
Rep. these 2 rows twice more.
Change to larger size needles.
Work in pat. from chart for front until row 26 has been completed. **
Change to brown and work 4 rows St. st.
Continuing in grey only, work even in St. st. until 102 rows St. st. have been completed, so ending with a p. row.
Shape back neck
Next row: K. 42, turn and leave remaining sts. on a spare needle.
Bind off 4 sts. at neck edge twice.
Bind off remaining 34 sts.
Return to remaining sts.
With RS facing, slip first 11 sts. on to a needle holder, join on yarn and k. to end.
P. 1 row.
Bind off 4 sts. at neck edge twice.
Bind off remaining 34 sts.

FRONT
Work as given for back from ** to **.
Now beg. at row 27, continue in pat. from chart until row 92 has been completed.
Shape front neck
Next row: K. 42, turn and leave remaining sts. on a spare needle.
Continuing in pat. following chart, dec. 1 st. at neck edge on every row until 34 sts. remain.

Cherubs modeled by Sarah Green

Work 5 rows even.
Bind off.
Return to remaining sts.
With RS facing, slip first 11 sts. to a
holder, join on yarn and k. to end.
Now complete 2nd side of neck to match
first, reversing all shaping.

SLEEVES
Using smaller size needles and grey, cast
on 39 sts.
Work 2"/5cm rib as given for back,
ending rib row 1.
Inc. row: Rib 6, M. 1, * rib 4, M. 1, rep.
from * to last 5 sts., rib 5: 47 sts.
Change to larger size needles.
Work in St. st. increasing 1 st. each end
of 5th row and then every 4th row until
there are 75 sts.
Work 15 rows even.
Bind off.

NECKBAND
Join left shoulder seam.
With RS facing using smaller size
needles and grey, pick up and k. 10 sts.
down right side of back neck, k. across
11 sts. from back neck holder, pick up
and k. 11 sts. up left side of back neck
and 14 sts. down left side of front neck,
k. across 11 sts. from front neck holder,
then pick up and k. 14 sts. up right side
of front neck: 71 sts.
Beg. k. row, work 3 rows rev. St. st.
Bind off knitwise.

TO MAKE UP
Block and press pieces lightly under a
damp cloth following instructions on ball
band.
Join right shoulder and neckband seam.
Sew in sleeves. Join side and sleeve
seams.

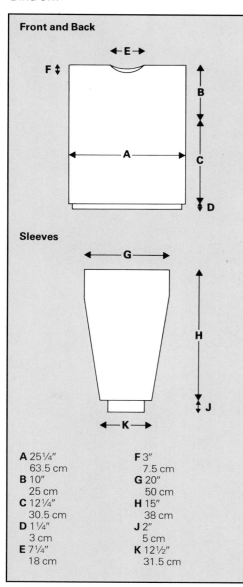

Front and Back

Sleeves

A 25¼"
  63.5 cm
B 10"
  25 cm
C 12¼"
  30.5 cm
D 1¼"
  3 cm
E 7¼"
  18 cm

F 3"
  7.5 cm
G 20"
  50 cm
H 15"
  38 cm
J 2"
  5 cm
K 12½"
  31.5 cm

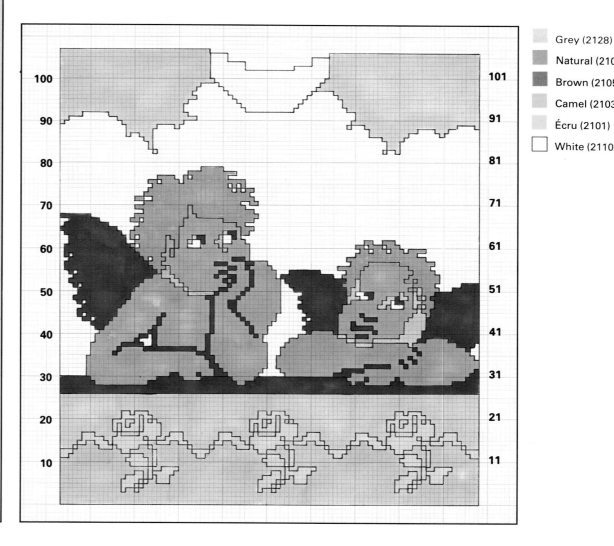

Grey (2128)
Natural (2102)
Brown (2105)
Camel (2103)
Écru (2101)
White (2110)

SHUNKOSAI
HOKUSHU
The Corrupt Official

During his life Hokushu was the most popular painter of actors in Osaka, mainly between 1810–1832. The scene depicted on the sweater is from the play *Keisei Sano no Funabashi* in which the actor, Ichikawa Ebijuro, is playing Miura Arajiro, a corrupt state official active under Prime Minister Tanuma. The strong features of the character have been worked into the sweater using a combination of embroidery and intarsia knitting. The yellow and grey chessboard background has the added detail of Japanese writing on the sleeves, worked in embroidery.

SIZES
To fit 36 (38, 40, 42, 44)"/90 (95, 100, 105, 110) cm chest loosely

MATERIALS
Schaffhauser Salvatore
7 (7, 8, 8, 9) × 50g balls in Silver Grey (shade 5197)

6 (6, 7, 7, 7) × 50g balls in Yellow (shade 44)

3 × 50g balls in Brown (shade 87)
1 × 50g ball each in Black (shade 121), White (shade 119) and Royal (shade 76)
A pair each of sizes 3 (3¼mm) and 6 (4mm) knitting needles
Stitch holders

GAUGE
23 sts. and 29 rows to 4"/10cm over St. st. worked on size 6 (4mm) needles.
Check your gauge

NOTES
Instructions for the larger sizes are given in parentheses ( ).
When working motif, use separate, small balls of yarn. When joining in a new color, leave an end of about 2"/5cm for weaving into the work later, and when changing color, twist the yarns together at the back of work to avoid making a hole.

BACK
** Using smaller size needles and silver grey, cast on 109 (115, 121, 127, 133) sts.

The Corrupt Official
modeled by Tim
Rice

Yellow (44)

Silver Grey (5197)

Brown (87)

Black (121)

White (119)

Royal (76)

Backstitch embroidery in Black (121)

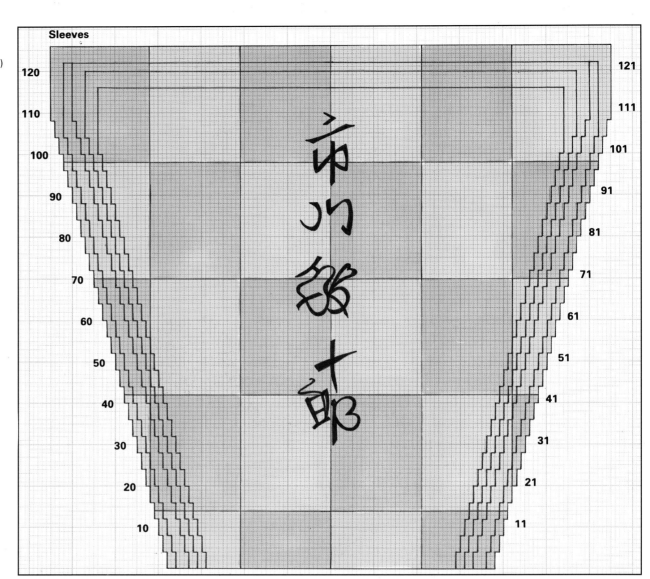

Sleeves

120 110 100 90 80 70 60 50 40 30 20 10

121 111 101 91 81 71 61 51 41 31 21 11

市川猿十郎

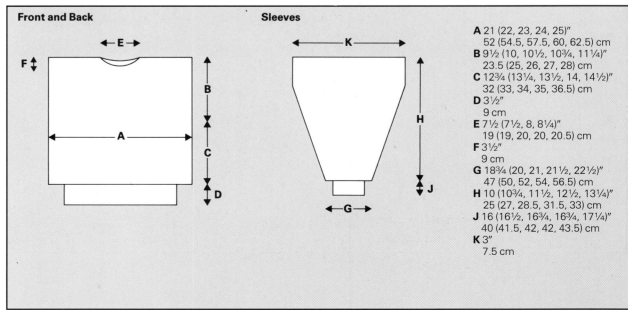

Front and Back

Sleeves

F
E
B
A
C
D

K
H
G
J

A 21 (22, 23, 24, 25)″
52 (54.5, 57.5, 60, 62.5) cm
B 9½ (10, 10½, 10¾, 11¼)″
23.5 (25, 26, 27, 28) cm
C 12¾ (13¼, 13½, 14, 14½)″
32 (33, 34, 35, 36.5) cm
D 3½″
9 cm
E 7½ (7½, 8, 8¼)″
19 (19, 20, 20, 20.5) cm
F 3½″
9 cm
G 18¾ (20, 21, 21½, 22½)″
47 (50, 52, 54, 56.5) cm
H 10 (10¾, 11½, 12½, 13¼)″
25 (27, 28.5, 31.5, 33) cm
J 16 (16½, 16¾, 16¾, 17¼)″
40 (41.5, 42, 42, 43.5) cm
K 3″
7.5 cm

Front

HOKUSHU

Rib row 1: K. 1, * p. 1, k. 1, rep. from * to end.
Rib row 2: P. 1, * k. 1, p. 1, rep. from * to end.
Rep. these 2 rows for 3½"/9cm, ending rib row 1.
Inc. row: Rib 4 (8, 10, 6, 6), M. 1, * rib 10 (10, 10, 11, 12), M. 1, rep. from * to last 5 (7, 11, 11, 7) sts., rib to end: 120 (126, 132, 138, 144) sts. **
Change to larger size needles.
Work large checks in silver grey and yellow as follows:
Row 1: K. 15 (18, 21, 24, 27) yellow, 45 silver grey, join in 2nd ball of yellow and k. 45 yellow, join in 2nd ball of silver grey and k. 15 (18, 21, 24, 27) silver grey.
Continue working in color blocks as established until 15 (19, 21, 25, 29) rows have been worked from beg.
Now reverse colors as follows:
Next row: P. 15 (18, 21, 24, 27) silver grey, 45 yellow, 45 silver grey, 15 (18, 21, 24, 27) yellow.
Continue working in color blocks as established until 56 rows have been worked in the reversed colors.
Reverse colors as before and work a further 56 rows, then reverse colors again and work 29 (33, 37, 39, 43) rows.
Shape back neck
Keeping color blocks as established, k. 47 (50, 53, 56, 59), turn and leave remaining sts. on a spare needle.
Work on these sts. only.
Next row: Bind off 4 (4, 5, 5, 6) sts., p. to end.
K. 1 row.
Next row: Bind off 5 sts., p. to end.
Bind off.
Return to remaining sts.
With RS facing, slip first 26 sts. to a holder, join yarn to next st. and k. to end.
P. 1 row.
Next row: Bind off 4 (4, 5, 5, 6) sts., k. to end.

P. 1 row.
Next row: Bind off 5 sts., k. to end.
Bind off.

FRONT
Work as given for back from ** to **.
Change to larger size needles.
Beg. at row 15 (11, 9, 5, 1) of chart, work in pat. until row 148 (152, 156, 158, 162) has been completed.
Shape neck
Continue in pat. following chart, k. 50 (53, 56, 59, 62), turn and leave remaining sts. on a spare needle.
Work on these sts. only.
Dec. 1 st. at neck edge of every row until 38 (41, 43, 46, 48) sts. remain.
Work 13 (13, 12, 12, 11) rows even.
Bind off.
Return to remaining sts.
With RS facing, slip first 20 sts. to a holder, rejoin yarn to next st. and work 2nd side of neck to match first side, reversing all shaping.
Using black, embroider features in backstitch on face as indicated on chart.

SLEEVES
Using smaller size needles and yellow, cast on 49 (53, 55, 61, 65) sts.
Work the 2 rib rows as given for back for 2¾"/7cm, ending rib row 1.
Inc. row: Rib 4 (6, 8, 10, 8), M. 1, * rib 5 (5, 4, 4, 5), M. 1, rep. from * to last 5 (7, 7, 11, 7) sts., rib to end: 58 (62, 66, 72, 76) sts.
Change to larger size needles.
Work in small check pat. from chart as follows:
Row 1: K. 8 (10, 12, 15, 17) silver grey, 21 yellow, 21 silver grey, 8 (10, 12, 15, 17) yellow.
Continue working from chart, increasing 1 st. each end of 5th row and then every 4th row until there are 108 (114, 120, 124, 130) sts.
Work 15 (15, 13, 17, 17) rows even.
Bind off.
Using black, work embroidery in backstitch as indicated on chart.

NECKBAND
Join left shoulder seam.
With RS facing, using smaller size needles and silver grey, pick up and k. 10 (10, 11, 11, 12) sts. down right back neck, k. across 26 sts. from holder, pick up and k. 9 (9, 10, 10, 11) sts. up left back neck, 24 (24, 25, 25, 25) sts. down left front neck, k. across 20 sts. from holder, pick up and k. 24 (24, 25, 25, 25) sts. up right front neck:
113 (113, 117, 117, 119) sts.
P. 1 row.
Work 8 rows in rib as given for back.
Bind off loosely in rib.

TO MAKE UP
Block and press pieces lightly under a damp cloth following ball instructions.
Join right shoulder and neckband seam.
Fold neckband in half to WS and slipstitch into place. Sew in sleeves, then join side and sleeve seams.

CLAUDE MONET
Poppy Fields

This little painting of Monet's wife, Camille, and son, Jean, walking through a field of poppies was created in 1873 and shown at the first Impressionist exhibition the following year. Camille and Jean appear twice in the painting, this detail drawing the eye to the hillside of bright red poppies.

The design has been worked around the sweater, including the raglan sleeves. The green background is in a pure wool tweed which gives a feeling of texture and tone without changing yarns. The poppies are worked in two shades of red, in knitting and embroidery, to give an illusion of depth.

SIZES
One size only to fit 32 to 38"/80 to 95cm chest

MATERIALS
Anny Blatt No. 4
8 × 50g balls in Green (shade 1567)
3 × 50g balls in Écru (shade 1298)
1 × 50g ball each in Dark Olive (shade 1308), Light Grey (shade 1295), Bright Red (shade 1309), Black (shade 1310), Cherry Red (shade 1287) and Blue (shade 1289)
A pair each of sizes 3 (3¼mm) and 6 (4mm) knitting needles.
Stitch holders

GAUGE
22 sts. and 30 rows to 4"/10cm over St. st. worked on size 6 (4mm) needles.
Check your gauge

NOTES
When working motif, use separate, small balls of yarn. When joining in a new color, leave an end of about 2"/5cm for weaving into the work later and when changing color, twist yarns together at back of work to avoid making a hole.

BACK
** Using smaller size needles and green, cast on 125 sts.
Rib row 1: K. 1, * p. 1, k. 1, rep. from * to end.
Rib row 2: P. 1, * k. 1, p. 1, rep. from * to end.
Rep. these 2 rows for 2¼"/6cm, increasing 1 st. at end of last row: 126 sts. **
Change to larger size needles.
Work 68 rows St. st.
Work in pat. from chart for back as follows:
Row 1: K. 43 green, 2 bright red, 2 green, 1 bright red, 78 green.
Row 2: P. 77 green, 2 bright red, 1 green, 2 bright red, 44 green.
Continue in pat. until row 22 has been completed.

Shape raglans
Continuing in pat. following chart, bind off 4 sts. at beg. of next 2 rows then dec. 1 st. each end of next row and then every other row until 48 sts. remain, ending with a p. row.

Shape neck
Next row: K. 2 tog., k. 10, turn and leave remaining sts. on a spare needle.
Next Row: Bind off 5 sts., p. to end.
Next row: K. 2 tog., k. to end: 5 sts.
Bind off.
Return to remaining sts.
With RS facing, slip first 24 sts. to a holder, join on yarn and k. to last 2 sts., k. 2 tog.

Poppy Fields
modeled by
Anneka Rice

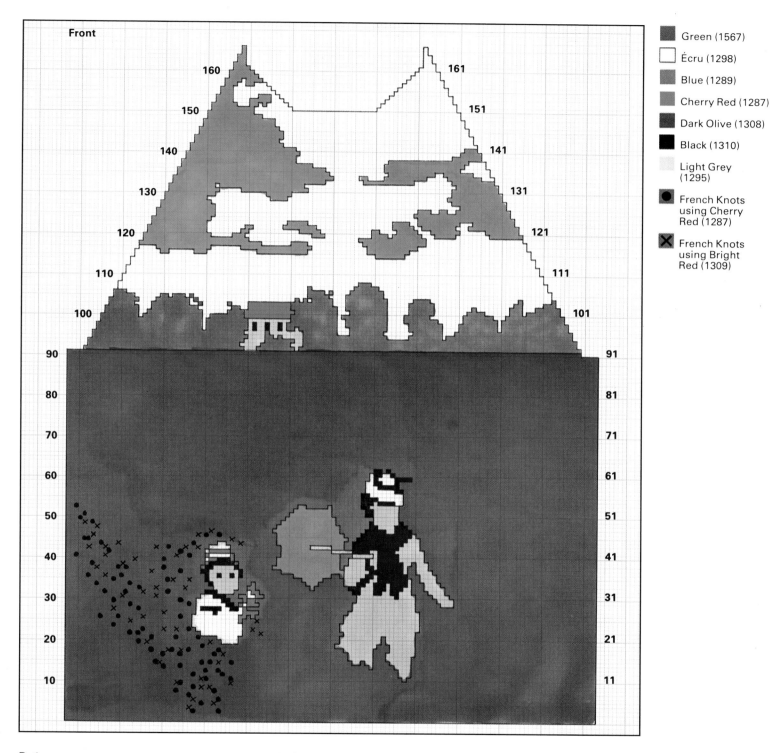

Front

160 161
150 151
140 141
130 131
120 121
110 111
100 101
90 91
80 81
70 71
60 61
50 51
40 41
30 31
20 21
10 11

Green (1567)

Écru (1298)

Blue (1289)

Cherry Red (1287)

Dark Olive (1308)

Black (1310)

Light Grey (1295)

● French Knots using Cherry Red (1287)

✕ French Knots using Bright Red (1309)

P. 1 row.
Next row: Bind off 5 sts., k. to last 2 sts., k. 2 tog.
P. 1 row.
Bind off.

FRONT
Work as given for back from ** to **.
Change to larger size needles.
Work in pat. from chart for front until row 90 has been completed.
Continuing in pat. following chart, shape raglan as given for back until 60 sts. remain, ending with a p. row.
Shape neck
Next row: Continuing in pat. following chart, k. 2 tog., k. 18, turn and leave remaining sts. on a holder.
Continuing to shape raglan edge as before, dec. 1 st. at neck edge every row until 3 sts. remain.
Dec. 1 st. at raglan edge only until 1 st. remains.
Fasten off.
Return to remaining sts.
With RS facing, slip first 20 sts. to a holder, join on yarn then continuing in pat. following chart, work 2nd side of neck to match first side, reversing all shaping.

47

CLAUDE MONET

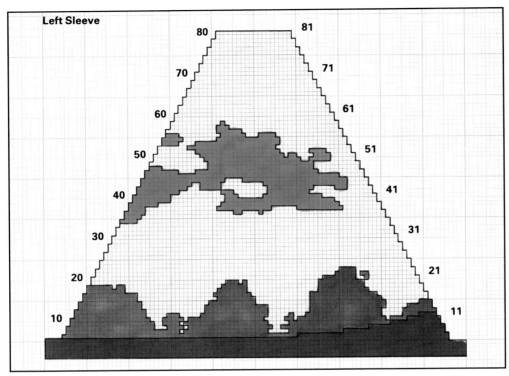

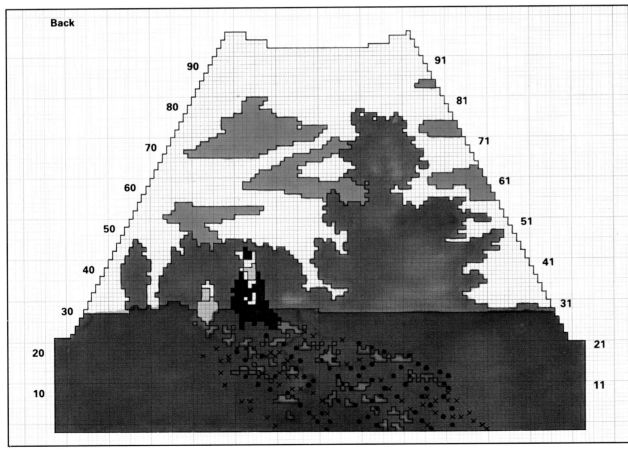

LEFT SLEEVE

Using smaller size needles and green, cast on 55 sts.

Work 2¼"/6cm in rib as given for back, ending with rib row 1.

Inc. row: Rib 2, M. 1, * rib 5, M. 1, rep. from * to last 3 sts., rib to end: 66 sts.

Change to larger size needles.

Working in St. st., inc. 1 st. each end of 5th row and then every 6th row until there are 100 sts., ending with a p. row.

Working in pat. from chart for left sleeve, work 4 rows.

Continuing in pat. following chart, work raglan shaping as given for back until 18 sts. remain, ending with a p. row.

Break off yarn and leave sts. on a holder.

RIGHT SLEEVE

Work as given for left sleeve until there are 84 sts., ending with a p. row.

Working in pat. from chart for right sleeve, continue shaping as given for left sleeve until there are 100 sts., then work even until row 52 has been completed.

Continuing in pat. following chart, work raglan shaping as given for back until 18 sts. remain, ending with a p. row.

Break off yarn and leave sts. on a holder.

NECKBAND

Join front and left back raglan seams. With RS facing and using smaller size needles and cream, pick up and k. 10 sts. down right side of back neck, k. across 24 sts. from holder, pick up and k. 11 sts. up left side of back neck, k. across 18 sts. of left sleeve, pick up and k. 15 sts. down left side of front neck, k. across 20 sts. from holder, pick up and k. 15 sts. up right side of front neck, then k. across 18 sts. of right sleeve: 131 sts.

P. 1 row.

Rib row 1: K. 1, * p. 1, k. 1, rep. from * to end.

Rib row 2: P. 1, * k. 1, p. 1, rep. from * to end.

Rep. these 2 rows once more, then rib row 1 again.

Bind off in rib.

TO MAKE UP

Block and press pieces lightly under a damp cloth following band instructions. Join right back raglan and neckband seam. Join side and sleeve seams. Embroider French Knots as on chart.

Right Sleeve

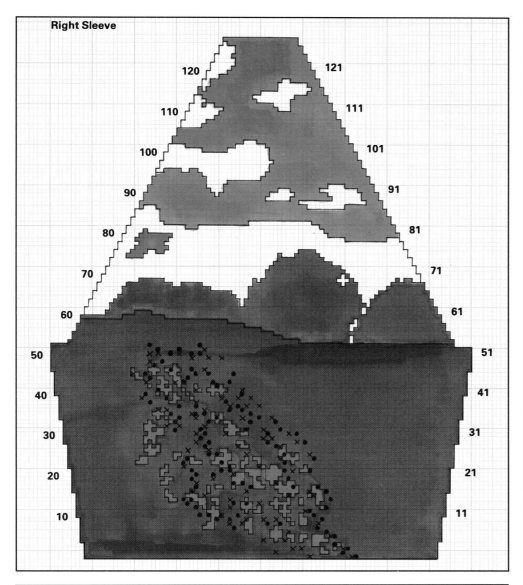

120 121
110 111
100 101
90 91
80 81
70 71
60 61
50 51
40 41
30 31
20 21
10 11

Front and Back

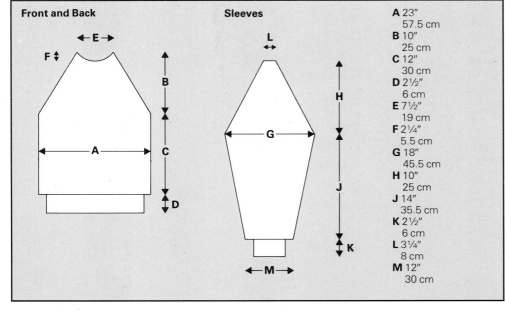

E
F
B
A
C
D

Sleeves

L
H
G
J
K
M

A 23″
57.5 cm
B 10″
25 cm
C 12″
30 cm
D 2½″
6 cm
E 7½″
19 cm
F 2¼″
5.5 cm
G 18″
45.5 cm
H 10″
25 cm
J 14″
35.5 cm
K 2½″
6 cm
L 3¼″
8 cm
M 12″
30 cm

EDGAR DEGAS
Racehorses at Longchamps

Degas painted this picture between 1873 and 1875. It shows the jockeys and their mounts approaching the start. He has chosen a quiet moment before the race begins, rather than the drama of galloping horses, as he is more concerned with the atmosphere than with documentary detail. The bright colors of the jockeys' shirts and caps provide a marked contrast to the dull green of the background. The main group of riders appears on the front of the garment and a group of more frisky horses gives added interest to the back.

SIZES
To fit 32 (34, 36, 38)"/80 (85, 90, 95) cm chest

MATERIALS
Schaffhauser Salvatore
8 × 50g balls in Light Green (shade 37)
3 × 50g balls in Light Beige (shade 73)
1 × 50g ball each in Dark Olive (shade 90), Blue (shade 43), Pink (shade 105), Brown (shade 322), Yellow (shade 44), Light Brown (shade 87) and Beige (shade 39)
A pair each of sizes 3 (3¼mm) and 6 (4mm) knitting needles
Stitch holders

GAUGE
22 sts. and 30 rows to 4"/10cm over St. st. worked on size 6 (4mm) needles.
Check your gauge

NOTES
Instructions for the larger sizes are given in parentheses ( ).
When working motif, use separate, small balls of yarn. When joining in a new color, leave an end of about 2"/5cm for weaving in later, and when changing color, twist yarns together at back of work to avoid making a hole.

BACK
** Using smaller size needles and light green, cast on 106 (112, 118, 124) sts.
K. 8 rows. **
Change to larger size needles.
Work in pat. from chart for back until row 134 (138, 140, 144) is complete.
Shape neck
Next row: K. 44 (47, 50, 53), turn and leave remaining sts. on a spare needle.
Bind off 5 sts. at beg. of next row.
Knit 1 row. Bind off 5 sts., work to end: 34 (37, 40, 43) sts.
Bind off.
Return to remaining sts.
With RS facing, slip first 18 sts. to a holder, join on yarn and k. to end.
P. 1 row.
Bind off 5 sts. at beg. of next row.
P. 1 row.
Bind off 5 sts., work to end.
Bind off.

FRONT
Work as given for back from ** to **.
Change to larger size needles.
Work in pat. from chart for front until row 120 (124, 126, 130) is complete.
Shape neck
Next row: K. 43 (46, 49, 52), turn and leave remaining sts. on a spare needle.
Dec. 1 st. at neck edge on every row until 34 (37, 40, 43) sts. remain.
Work 8 rows even.
Bind off.
Return to remaining sts.

Racehorses at Longchamps modeled by Jilly Cooper

EDGAR DEGAS

Light Green (37)

Light Beige (73)

Blue (43)

Dark Olive (90)

Brown (322)

Light Brown (87)

Yellow (44)

Pink (105)

Beige (39)

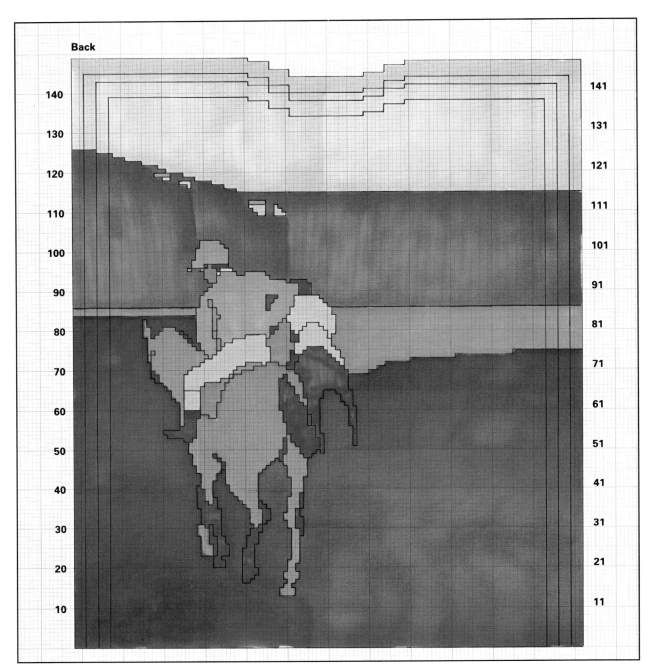

Back

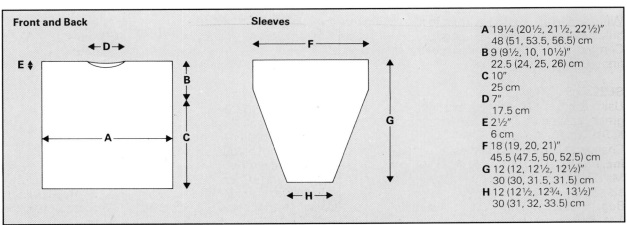

Front and Back

Sleeves

A 19¼ (20½, 21½, 22½)"
48 (51, 53.5, 56.5) cm
B 9 (9½, 10, 10½)"
22.5 (24, 25, 26) cm
C 10"
25 cm
D 7"
17.5 cm
E 2½"
6 cm
F 18 (19, 20, 21)"
45.5 (47.5, 50, 52.5) cm
G 12 (12, 12½, 12½)"
30 (30, 31.5, 31.5) cm
H 12 (12½, 12¾, 13½)"
30 (31, 32, 33.5) cm

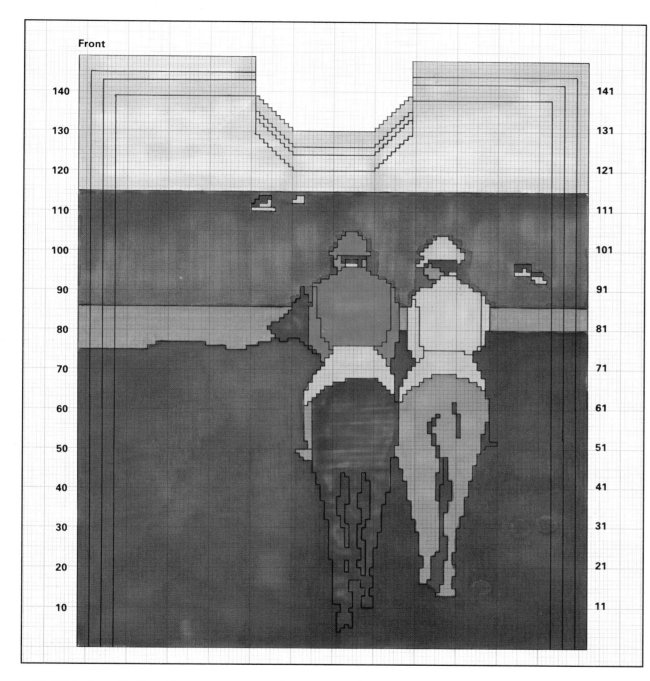

Front

With RS facing, slip first 20 sts. to a holder, join on yarn and k. to end. Complete 2nd side of neck to match first, reversing all shaping.

SLEEVES
Using smaller size needles and light green, cast on 61 (63, 65, 69) sts.
K. 8 rows.
Change to larger size needles.
Inc. row: K. 11 (11, 13, 15), M. 1, * k. 10, M. 1, rep. from * to last 10 (12, 12, 14) sts., k. to end: 66 (68, 70, 74) sts.
Beg. p. row, continue in St. st. increasing 1 st. each end of every 4th row until

there are 100 (104, 110, 116) sts.
Work 21 (17, 13, 9) rows even.
Bind off.

NECKBAND
Join left shoulder seam.
With RS facing and using smaller size needles and light beige, pick up and k. 18 sts. down right side of back neck, k. across 18 sts. from holder, pick up and k. 19 sts. up left side of back neck and 25 sts. down left side of front neck, k. across 20 sts. from holder, then pick up and k. 25 sts. up right side of front neck: 125 sts.

P. 1 row.
Rib row 1: K. 1, * p. 1, k. 1, rep. from * to end.
Rib row 2: P. 1, * k. 1, p. 1, rep. from * to end.
Rep. these 2 rows once more, then work rib row 1 again.
Bind off in rib.

TO MAKE UP
Block and press pieces lightly under a damp cloth following band instructions.
Join right shoulder and neckband seam.
Sew in sleeves, then join side and sleeve seams.

PAUL GAUGUIN

Tahitian Women on the Beach

This complete painting of 1891 depicts two statuesque women lazing on a Tahitian beach, both self-absorbed and silent. The scene is timeless and languorous. The background is made up of bands of flat color dividing the canvas vertically and pushing the figures forward, emphasizing their monumental solidity. These bands of color are featured all round the sweater. Gauguin's work lends itself well to the bright chunky cottons used in these designs.

SIZES
To fit 32 (34, 36, 38)"/80 (85, 90, 95) cm chest

MATERIALS
Scheepjeswool Mayflower Cotton Helarsgarn
8 × 50g balls in Yellow (shade 909)
8 × 50g balls in Pale Yellow (shade 908)
5 × 50g balls in Green (shade 965)
1 × 50g ball each in Black (915), Red (910), White (902) and Beige (936)
A pair each of sizes 6 (4mm) and 7 (4½mm) knitting needles
One size 6 (4mm) circular knitting needle
Raglan shoulder pads
One 2"/5cm red button
Stitch holders

GAUGE
18 sts. and 25 rows to 4"/10cm over St. st. worked on size 7 (4½mm) needles.
Check your gauge

NOTES
Instructions for the larger sizes are given in parentheses ().
When working motif, use separate, small balls of yarn. When joining in a new color, leave an end of about 2"/5cm for weaving in later, and when changing color, twist yarns together at back of work to avoid making a hole.

BACK
Using smaller size needles and yellow, cast on 109 (113, 119, 123) sts.
Rib row 1: K. 1, * p. 1, k. 1, rep. from * to end.

Rib row 2: P. 1, * k. 1, p. 1, rep. from * to end.
Rep. these 2 rows twice more.
Change to larger size needles.
Dec. row: K. 1 (3, 6, 8), k. 2 tog., * k. 5, k. 2 tog., rep. from * to last 1 (3, 6, 8) sts., k. to end: 93 (97, 103, 107) sts.
Work 37 (39, 41, 45) rows St. st.
Working from chart for back, place pat. as follows:
Row 1: P. 26 (28, 31, 33) yellow, 2 black, 6 yellow, 2 black, 4 yellow, 2 black, 2 yellow, 2 black, 4 yellow, 2 black, 2 yellow, 2 black, 6 yellow, 2 black, 6 yellow, 2 black, 21 (23, 26, 28) yellow.
Continue working from chart in this way until row 15 has been completed.
Change to pale yellow and continue in pat. from chart until row 45 has been completed.
Shape raglans
Continuing in pat. following chart, dec. 1 st. each end of every row until 75 (79, 81, 85) sts. remain, then dec. 1 st. each end of every 3rd row until row 65 of chart has been completed.
Continue shaping raglans as before working 4 more rows in pale yellow, then

PAUL GAUGUIN

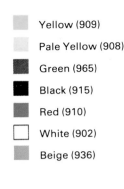

Yellow (909)
Pale Yellow (908)
Green (965)
Black (915)
Red (910)
White (902)
Beige (936)

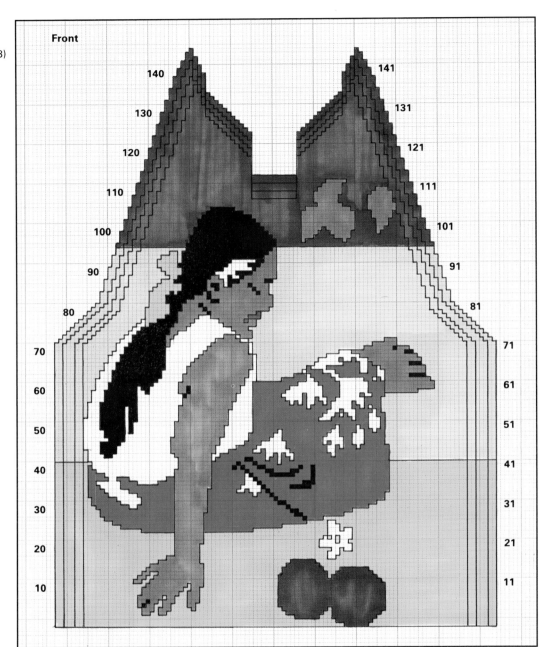

Front

140 141
130 131
120 121
110 111
100 101
90 91
80 81
70 71
60 61
50 51
40 41
30 31
20 21
10 11

Back

60 61
50 51
40 41
30 31
20 21
10 11

working in green until 39 (41, 43, 47) sts.
remain.
Shape neck
1st size only
P. 1 row.
4th size only
K. 1 row. Dec. 1 st. at each end of the
next row.
All sizes
Next row: K. 13 (14, 15, 16) sts., turn and
leave remaining sts. on a spare needle.
Next row: Bind off 5 (5, 6, 6) sts., p. to
last 2 sts., p. 2 tog.
K. 1 row.
Next row: Bind off 5 (6, 6, 7) sts.,
p. 2 tog. and fasten off.

Return to remaining sts.
With RS facing, slip first 13 sts. to a
holder, join yarn to next st. and k. to end.
Next row: P. 2 tog., p. to end.
Next row: Bind off 5 (5, 6, 6) sts., k. to
end.
Next row: P. 2 tog., p. to end.
Bind off.

FRONT
Work as given for back until 10 (12, 14,
18) rows of St. st. have been completed.
Work in pat. from chart for front as
follows:
Row 1: K. 24 (26, 29, 31) yellow, 6
green, 63 (65, 68, 70) yellow.

Continue in pat. in this way until row 72
has been completed.
Shape raglans
Continuing in pat. following chart, work
raglan shaping as given for back until 57
(61, 63, 65) sts. remain, ending with a
p. row.
1st and 4th sizes only
Next row: K. 23 (27) sts., turn.
2nd and 3rd sizes only
Next row: K. 2 tog., k. 23 (24) sts., turn.
All sizes
Leave remaining sts. on a spare needle.
Keeping neck edge straight, continue in
pat. from chart decreasing at raglan edge
as before until row 126 has been completed.

Keeping raglan shaping as before, dec. 1 st. at neck edge on every row until 5 sts. remain, then dec. at raglan edge only until 1 st. remains. Fasten off.
Return to remaining sts.
With RS facing, rejoin yarn and bind off the first 11 sts. then complete the 2nd side of neck to match first, reversing all shaping.

SLEEVES
Using smaller size needles and yellow, cast on 51 (55, 59, 63) sts.
Work 6 rows rib as given for back.
Change to larger size needles.
Working in St. st., inc. 1 st. each end of first row and then every 4th row until there are 73 (77, 81, 85) sts.
Work 1 (3, 5, 7) rows even.
Change to pale yellow; work 30 rows St. st.

Shape raglan
Dec. 1 st. each end of next 6 (8, 10, 12) rows, then each end of every 3rd row until 49 (49, 51, 53) sts. remain.

For 1st, 3rd and 4th sizes only
Work 2 (1, 2) rows even.

All sizes
Change to green and continue to dec. on every 3rd row as before until 33 sts. remain.
Work 2 rows.
Next row: K. 2 tog. tbl., k. 13, sl. 1, k. 2 tog., psso., k. 13, k. 2 tog.
Continue to work raglan shaping as before *and at the same time* shape shoulder by working sl. 1, k. 2 tog., psso. at center of every other row until 7 sts. remain.
Continue to dec. at raglan edges only until 5 sts. remain.
Work 2 rows even.
Break off yarn and leave sts. on a holder.

NECKBAND
Join raglan seams.
With RS facing, using circular needle and green, pick up and k. 16 (17, 18, 19) sts. up right side of front neck, k. across 5 sts. of first sleeve, pick up and k. 10 (12, 12, 13) sts. down right side of back neck, k. across 13 sts. from holder, pick up and k. 10 (12, 12, 13) sts. up left side of back neck, k. across 5 sts. of second sleeve, then pick up and k. 16 (17, 18, 19) sts. down left side of front neck: 75 (81, 83, 87) sts.
Working back and forth as with straight needles, p. 1 row.
Work 6 rows in rib as given for back.
Bind off in rib.

BUTTON BORDER
With RS facing and using smaller size

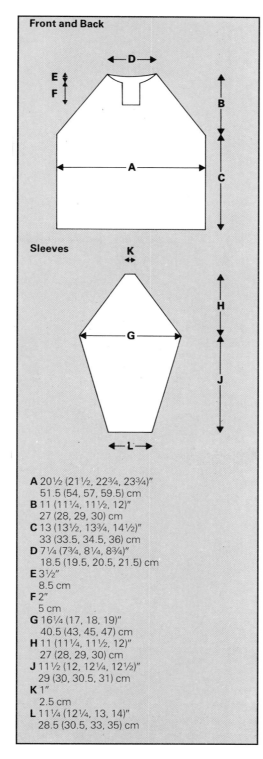

Front and Back

Sleeves

A 20½ (21½, 22¾, 23¾)"
  51.5 (54, 57, 59.5) cm
B 11 (11¼, 11½, 12)"
  27 (28, 29, 30) cm
C 13 (13½, 13¾, 14½)"
  33 (33.5, 34.5, 36) cm
D 7¼ (7¾, 8¼, 8¾)"
  18.5 (19.5, 20.5, 21.5) cm
E 3½"
  8.5 cm
F 2"
  5 cm
G 16¼ (17, 18, 19)"
  40.5 (43, 45, 47) cm
H 11 (11¼, 11½, 12)"
  27 (28, 29, 30) cm
J 11½ (12, 12¼, 12½)"
  29 (30, 30.5, 31) cm
K 1"
  2.5 cm
L 11¼ (12¼, 13, 14)"
  28.5 (30.5, 33, 35) cm

needles and green, pick up and k. 15 sts. down left side of front opening.
Work 15 rows in rib as given for back.
Bind off in rib.

BUTTONHOLE BORDER
Picking up 15 sts. up right side of front opening, work as given for button border until 7 rows of rib have been completed.

Next row: Rib 6, bind off 7, rib 2.
Next row: Rib 2, cast on 7, rib 6.
Work 6 more rows in rib.
Bind off in rib.

TO MAKE UP
Block and press pieces lightly under a damp cloth following instructions on ball band. Matching bands of color, join side and sleeve seams. Overlap buttonhole border over button border and stitch row ends into place. Sew on button. Sew in shoulder pads.

PAUL GAUGUIN
When Will You Marry?

The innocence of young girls discussing their future is captured beautifully by Gauguin in this painting of 1892. They seem to have forgotten their work momentarily to pour out their innermost secrets. The rest of the world carries on, as the people in the far distance show.

The bold, naïve figures in the painting have all the attention in this dress. They have almost been sculpted to the front of the garment while the flatteringly low back retains simplicity.

SIZES
To fit 32 (34, 36)"/80 (85, 90) cm chest

MATERIALS
Scheepjeswool Mayflower Cotton Helarsgarn
6 × 50g balls in Green (shade 965)
4 × 50g balls in Yellow (shade 909)
2 × 50g balls each in Black (shade 915), Red (shade 910), White (shade 902), Beige (shade 936), Pink (shade 1006), Grey (shade 964) and Blue (shade 906)
A pair each of sizes 6 (4mm) and 7 (4½mm) knitting needles
Stitch holders
3 medium buttons

GAUGE
18 sts. and 25 rows to 4"/10cm over St. st. worked on size 7 (4½mm) needles.
Check your gauge

NOTES
Instructions for the larger sizes are given in parentheses ( ).
When working motif, use separate, small balls of yarn. When joining in a new color, leave an end of about 2"/5cm for weaving in later, and when changing color, twist yarns together at back of work to avoid making a hole.

BACK
First half
** Using smaller size needles and green, cast on 29 (33, 37) sts.
Rib row 1: K. 1, * p. 1, k. 1, rep. from * to end.
Rib row 2: P. 1, * k. 1, p. 1, rep. from * to end.
Rep. these 2 rows twice more.

Change to larger size needles.
Dec. row: K. 6 (5, 6), k. 2 tog., * k. 6 (5, 4), k. 2 tog., rep. from * to last 5 sts., k. to end: 26 (29, 32) sts.
Proceeding in St. st., work 56 rows, ending with a p. row. **
Break off yarn and leave sts. on a spare needle.

Second half
Work as given for first half from ** to ** but do not break off yarn.
Next row: K. 26 (29, 32), turn and cast on 2 sts., turn and k. 26 (29, 32) sts. from spare needle: 54 (60, 66) sts.
Work even until 88 rows St. st. have been completed from beg., ending with a p. row.

Shape sides
Inc. 1 st. each end of next row and then every 10th row 5 times but when working the last inc. row *at the same time* work row 1 from chart as follows:
Row 1: With yellow inc. in first st., k. 7 (10, 13), 8 green, 6 yellow, 3 green, 3 yellow, 2 green, 8 yellow, 6 green, 4 yellow, 7 green, 6 (9, 12) yellow, then with yellow inc. in last st.: 64 (70, 76) sts.
Continue in pat. from chart, shaping

When Will You
Marry? modeled by
Helena Springs

PAUL GAUGUIN

Legend:
- Green (965)
- Beige (936)
- Black (915)
- White (902)
- Pink (1006)
- Red (910)
- Grey (964)
- Blue (906)
- Yellow (909)

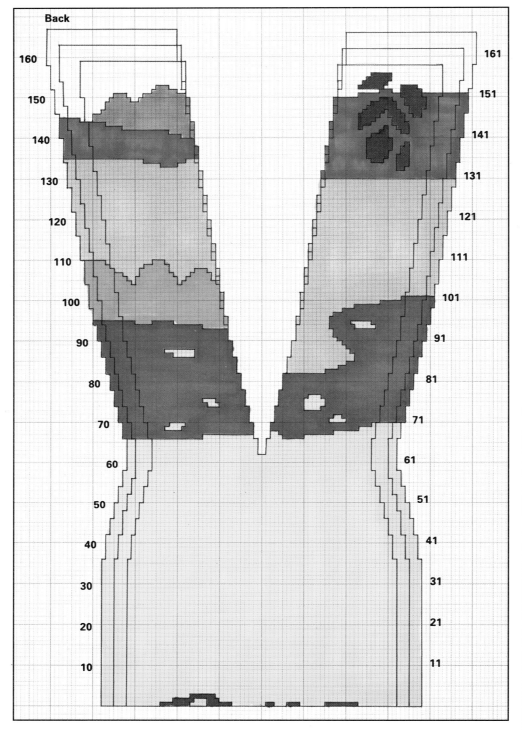

Back

160 150 140 130 120 110 100 90 80 70 60 50 40 30 20 10

161 151 141 131 121 111 101 91 81 71 61 51 41 31 21 11

Front

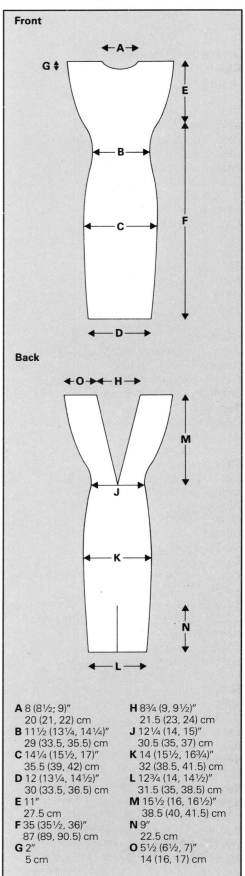

Front

A

G

E

B

F

C

D

Back

O H

M

J

K

N

L

A 8 (8½; 9)"	**H** 8¾ (9, 9½)"
20 (21, 22) cm	21.5 (23, 24) cm
B 11½ (13¼, 14¼)"	**J** 12¼ (14, 15)"
29 (33.5, 35.5) cm	30.5 (35, 37) cm
C 14¼ (15½, 17)"	**K** 14 (15½, 16¾)"
35.5 (39, 42) cm	32 (38.5, 41.5) cm
D 12 (13¼, 14½)"	**L** 12¾ (14, 14½)"
30 (33.5, 36.5) cm	31.5 (35, 38.5) cm
E 11"	**M** 15½ (16, 16½)"
27.5 cm	38.5 (40, 41.5) cm
F 35 (35½, 36)"	**N** 9"
87 (89, 90.5) cm	22.5 cm
G 2"	**O** 5½ (6½, 7)"
5 cm	14 (16, 17) cm

sides as indicated until row 62 has been completed.

Divide for neck
Next row: Continuing in pat. following chart, k. 25 (29, 31), bind off 2 sts., k. to end.
Next row: P. 25 (29, 31) sts., turn and leave remaining sts. on a spare needle. Work on these sts. only for left side of back.
Work 2 rows even.
Continuing to work from chart, inc. 1 st. at side edge and dec. 1 st. at neck edge on next row and then every 4th row 6 (7, 8) times, then every 6th row 10 times.
Work even until row 166 has been completed.
Bind off.
With WS facing, rejoin yarn to remaining sts. and complete to match first side of back, reversing all shaping.

FRONT
Using smaller size needles and green, cast on 67 (73, 79) sts.
Work 6 rows in rib as given for back.
Change to larger size needles.
Dec. row: K. 5 (4, 7), k. 2 tog., * k. 4 (5, 5), k. 2 tog., rep. from * to last 6 (4, 7) sts., k. to end: 57 (63, 69) sts.
Proceeding in St. st., work 88 rows even.
Shape sides
Inc. 1 st. each end of next row and following 10th row: 61 (67, 73) sts.
Work 9 rows even.
Place motif
Increasing 1 st. each end of first row, work from chart as follows:
Row 1: For 3rd size only k. 3 beige, then **for all sizes** k. 30 (33, 33) green, 4 beige, 29 (32, 35) green.
Row 2: P. 29 (32, 35) green, 5 beige, 29 (31, 31) green, then **for 2nd and 3rd sizes only** p. 1 (4) beige.
Continue working from chart, shaping sides as indicated until row 166 (170, 174) has been completed.
Shape neck
Continuing in pat. following chart, k. 38 (43, 46), turn and leave remaining sts. on a spare needle.
Work on these sts. only.
Next row: Bind off 6 sts., p. to end.
K. 1 row.
Next row: Bind off 6 sts., p. to end.
Next row: Inc. in first st., k. to last 2 sts., k. 2 tog.
Now dec. 1 st. at neck edge on every row until 25 (29, 31) sts. remain.
Work 6 (5, 4) rows even.
Bind off.

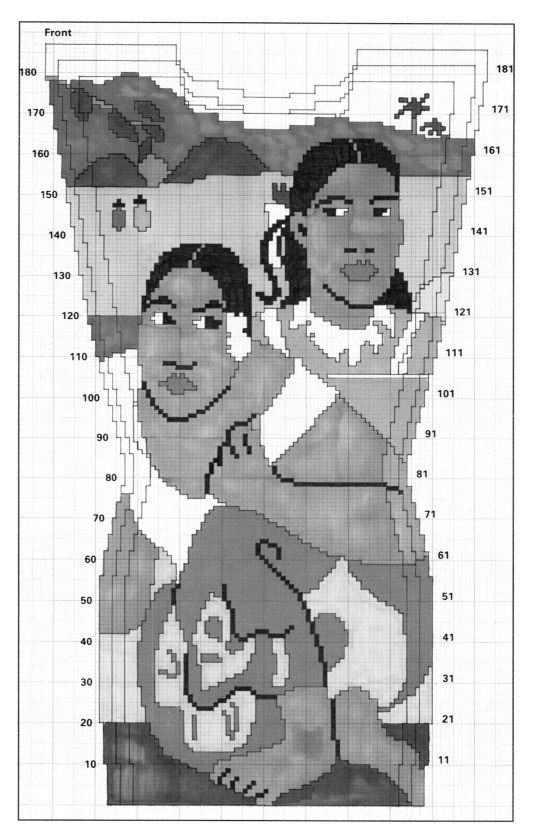

Return to remaining sts.
With RS facing, slip first 11 sts. to a holder, rejoin yarn to next st. and k. to end, maintaining chart pat.
Now complete second side of neck to match first, reversing all shaping.

FRONT NECKBAND
With RS facing, using smaller size needles and white, pick up and k. 25 (26, 27) sts. down left side of neck, k. across 11 sts. of center front then pick up and k. 25 (26, 27) sts. up right side of neck: 61 (63, 65) sts.
P. 1 row, then work 4 rows in rib as given for back.
Bind off in rib.

BACK NECKBAND
With RS facing, using smaller size needles and white, pick up and k. 50 (52, 54) sts. down right side of back neck, 1 st. at base of "V" and 50 (52, 54) sts. up left side of back neck: 101 (105, 109) sts.
P. 1 row, then beg. with k. 1, work 1 row in rib.
Next row: Rib 47 (49, 51) sts., k. 3 tog. tbl., p. 1, k. 3 tog., rib 47 (49, 51). Work 2 more rows in rib.
Bind off in rib.

ARMHOLE BORDERS
Join shoulder and neckband seams. With RS facing, using smaller size needles and white, pick up and k. 59 (61, 63) sts. evenly round armhole.
P. 1 row, then work 4 rows in rib.
Bind off in rib.

RIGHT BUTTON BAND
With RS facing, using smaller size needles and green, pick up and k. 37 sts. up right side of slit at back of skirt.
P. 1 row, then work 5 rows in rib.
Bind off in rib.

LEFT BUTTONHOLE BAND
Work as given for right button band, working buttonholes on 2nd rib row as follows:
Buttonhole row: Rib 6, bind off 4 sts., * rib 8, bind off 4 sts., rep. from * to last 3 sts., rib to end.
Next row: Rib to end, casting on 4 sts. over those bound off in previous row. Work 2 more rows in rib, then bind off in rib.

TO MAKE UP
Block and press pieces lightly under a damp cloth following instructions on ball band.
Join side seams. Sew row-ends of button and buttonhole bands in place. Sew on buttons.

PAUL GAUGUIN

Tahitian Women Bathing

The painting (1892–3) shows the acceptance by Tahitians of this unconventional Parisian artist – they carry on with their bathing seemingly oblivious of Gauguin's careful scrutiny of their everyday lives. He painted his greatest works in Tahiti having found the tropical paradise of his dreams. This summer dress is shaped to reflect the voluptuous curves of the main figure. The back of the dress shows the seated figure – the only one not joining in the fun.

SIZES
To fit 32 (34, 36)"/80 (85, 90) cm chest

MATERIALS
Scheepjeswool Mayflower Cotton Helarsgarn
4 × 50g balls in Green (shade 965)
2 × 50g balls each in Beige (shade 936), Black (shade 915), White (shade 902) and Blue (shade 906)
A pair each of sizes 6 (4mm) and 7 (4½mm) knitting needles
One size G (4½mm) crochet hook

GAUGE
18 sts. and 25 rows to 4"/10cm over St. st. worked on size 7 (4½mm) needles.
Check your gauge

NOTES
Instructions for the larger sizes are given in parentheses ( ).
When working motif, use separate, small balls of yarn. When joining in a new color, leave an end of about 2"/5cm for weaving in later, and when changing color, twist yarns together at back of work to avoid making a hole.

BACK
Using smaller size needles and green, cast on 69 (77, 83) sts.
Rib row 1: K. 1, * p. 1, k. 1, rep. from * to end.
Rib row 2: P. 1, * k. 1, p. 1, rep. from * to end.
Rep. these 2 rows twice more.
Change to larger size needles.
Dec. row: K. 6 (2, 6), k. 2 tog., * k. 5, k. 2 tog., rep. from * to last 5 (3, 5) sts., k. to end: 60 (66, 72) sts.
Proceeding in St. st., work 20 rows.
Inc. 1 st. each end of next row and following 10th row: 64 (70, 76) sts.
Work even for 26 rows.
Place motif from chart as follows:
Row 1: P. 32 (35, 38) green, p. 6 blue, p. 26 (29, 32) green.
Row 2: K. 23 (26, 29) green, k. 14 blue, k. 27 (30, 33) green.
Beg. from row 3, continue working from chart, shaping sides as indicated until row 48 as been completed.
Using green, work 3 rows even.
Inc. 1 st. each end of next row and then every 4th row until there are 64 (72, 76) sts.
P. 1 row.
Change to blue.
1st size only
Work 2 rows.
Inc. 1 st. each end of next row: 66 sts.
All sizes
Work 3 (6, 10) rows even.
Shape armholes
Bind off 10 (10, 11) sts. at beg. of next 2 rows: 46 (52, 54) sts.
Bind off 3 sts. at beg. of next 2 rows and 2 sts. at beg. of following 2 rows.
Dec. 1 st. each end of next row and then

PAUL GAUGUIN

every other row until 26 (32, 38) sts.
remain.
Change to green and continue to dec. 1
st. at each end of every other row until
12 (14, 16) sts. remain, ending with a p.
row. Then inc. 1 st. at each end of the
next and every following alternate row
until there are 20 (22, 24) sts. ending
with a p. row.

Shape neck
Inc. in first st., k. 8 (9, 10), bind off next 2
sts., k. to last st., inc. in last st.
Next row: P. 8 (9, 10), k. 2 tog., turn and
leave remaining sts. on a spare needle.
Work on these sts. only for left back.
Next row: Bind off 2 (3, 4) sts., k. to last
st., inc. in last st: 8 sts.
P. 1 row.
Continue on these 8 sts., dec. 1 st. at
neck edge and inc. 1 st. at armhole edge
every other row 6 (4, 2) times.
P. 1 row.
Change to blue and continue to inc. and
dec. as before 2 (4, 6) times.
Work 5 rows even.
Bind off.
Return to remaining sts.
With WS facing, rejoin green and bind off
first 2 (3, 4) sts., p. to end.
Inc. 1 st. at armhole edge and dec. 1 st. at
neck edge every other row 6 (4, 2) times.
P. 1 row.
Change to blue and continuing to shape
as before, complete to match the first
side.

FRONT
Using smaller size needles and green,
cast on 75 (81, 87) sts.
Work 6 rows in rib as given for back.
Change to larger size needles.
Dec. row: K. 1 (4, 7), k. 2 tog., * k. 5,
k. 2 tog., rep. from * to last 2 (5, 8) sts., k.
to end: 64 (70, 76) sts.
Proceeding in St. st., work 11 rows.
Place motif from chart as follows:
Row 1: K. 20 (23, 26) green, 4 beige,
joining in second ball of green k. 8 green,
joining in second ball of beige k. 5 beige,
joining in third ball of green k. 27 (30, 33)
green.
Row 2: P. 26 (29, 32) green, 7 beige, 6
green, 6 beige, 19 (22, 25) green.
Beg. row 3, continue working from chart,
shaping sides and armholes as indicated,
until row 138 (142, 146) has been
completed.
Shape neck
Continuing in pat. following chart, k. 22
(23, 24), turn and leave remaining sts. on
a spare needle.
Work on these sts. only.

2nd size only
Bind off 3 sts. at beg. of next row.
P. 1 row.
All sizes
Bind off 2 sts. at neck edge every other
row until 8 sts. remain.
Work 22 (20, 18) rows even.

Bind off.
Return to remaining sts.
With RS facing, join on yarn and bind off
the first 16 sts., then continuing in pat.
following chart, complete second side of
neck to match first side, reversing all
shaping.

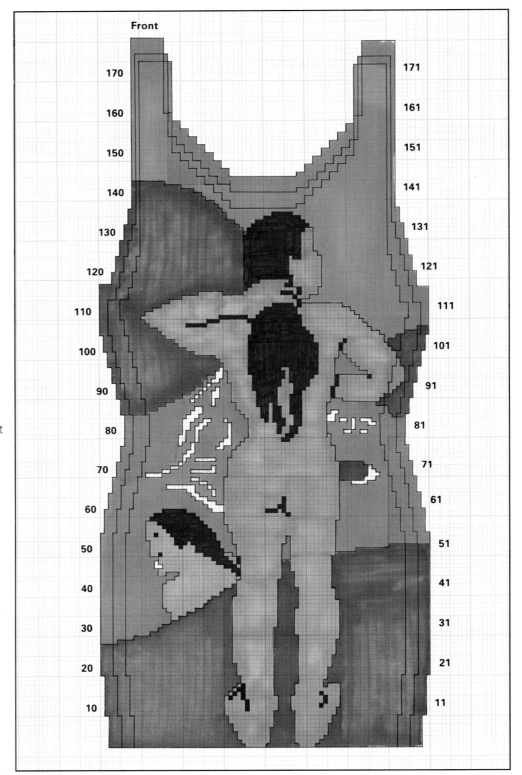

Front

170 171
160 161
150 151
140 141
130 131
120 121
110 111
100 101
90   91
80   81
70   71
60   61
50   51
40   41
30   31
20   21
10   11

Green (965)
Blue (906)
White (902)
Black (915)
Beige (936)

Tahitian Women
Bathing modeled
by Cherry Gillespie

PAUL GAUGUIN

NECK AND ARMHOLE EDGING
Join shoulder seams.
Using crochet hook and blue, work 1 round of single crochet evenly round neck and armhole edges.

TO MAKE UP
Block and press pieces lightly under a damp cloth following instructions on ball band.
Join side seams.

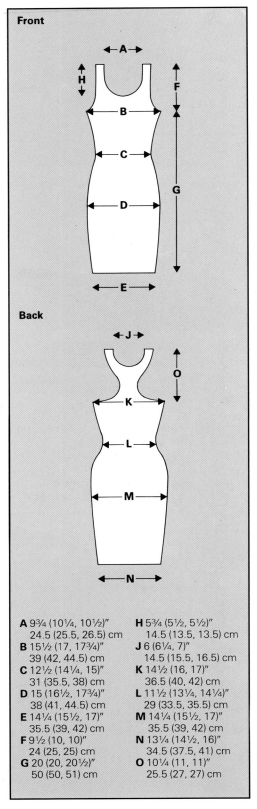

Front

Back

A 9¾ (10¼, 10½)" 24.5 (25.5, 26.5) cm	**H** 5¾ (5½, 5½)" 14.5 (13.5, 13.5) cm
B 15½ (17, 17¾)" 39 (42, 44.5) cm	**J** 6 (6¼, 7)" 14.5 (15.5, 16.5) cm
C 12½ (14¼, 15)" 31 (35.5, 38) cm	**K** 14½ (16, 17)" 36.5 (40, 42) cm
D 15 (16½, 17¾)" 38 (41, 44.5) cm	**L** 11½ (13¼, 14¼)" 29 (33.5, 35.5) cm
E 14¼ (15½, 17)" 35.5 (39, 42) cm	**M** 14¼ (15½, 17)" 35.5 (39, 42) cm
F 9½ (10, 10)" 24 (25, 25) cm	**N** 13¼ (14½, 16)" 34.5 (37.5, 41) cm
G 20 (20, 20½)" 50 (50, 51) cm	**O** 10¼ (11, 11)" 25.5 (27, 27) cm

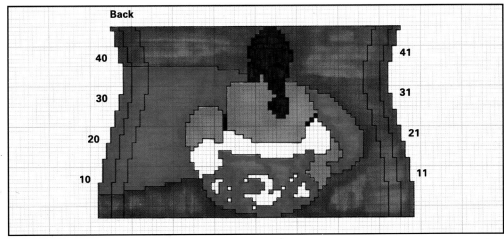

Back

HENRI DE TOULOUSE-LAUTREC

Moulin Rouge-
La Goulue

his was Lautrec's first poster, painted in 1891. La Goulue, with her distinct top-knot, flashes her frilly petticoats behind the emaciated silhouette of Boneless Valentin. The customers of the club are shown merely as a jaunty row of hats.

This jacket is entirely knitted in intarsia with features of Boneless Valentin and La Goulue worked in embroidery. The lettering has been limited to the sleeves and the back of the jacket.

SIZES
To fit 32 (34, 36, 38, 40)"/80 (85, 90, 95, 100) cm chest loosely

MATERIALS
Hayfield Grampian D.K.
7 (7, 8, 8, 8) × 50g balls Camel (shade 033018)
3 × 50g balls Cream (shade 033015)
2 × 50g balls Black (shade 033024)
1 × 50g ball each of Thistle (shade 033123), Scarlet (shade 033012), Fudge (shade 033017) and Daffodil (shade 033073)

A pair each of sizes 3 (3¼mm) and 6 (4mm) knitting needles
5 large red buttons
Shoulder pads (optional)

GAUGE
22 sts. and 29 rows to 4"/10cm over St. st. worked on size 6 (4mm) needles.
Check your gauge

NOTES
Instructions for the larger sizes are given in parentheses ( ).
When working motif, use separate, small balls of yarn. When joining in a new color, leave an end of about 2"/5cm for weaving in later, and when changing color, twist yarns together at back of work to avoid making a hole.

BACK
Using smaller size needles and thistle, cast on 115 (121, 125, 131, 137) sts.
Rib row 1: K. 1, * p. 1, k. 1, rep. from * to end.
Rib row 2: P. 1, * k. 1, p. 1, rep. from * to end.
Change to cream and rep. these 2 rows

12 times, then changing colors work 3 rows thistle and 3 rows black increasing 1 st. at center of last row.
Change to larger size needles and camel. Work 82 (88, 96, 100, 104) rows even.
Place motif from chart as follows:
Row 1: K. 89 (92, 94, 97, 100) camel, 4 scarlet, 10 camel, 4 scarlet, 9 (12, 14, 17, 20) camel.
Continue in pat. from chart until row 20 has been completed.
Shape armholes
Continuing in pat. following chart, bind off 6 sts. at beg. of next 2 rows.
Continue working from chart until row 66 has been completed.
Now working in camel only, work 34 (38, 38, 40, 40) rows even.
Shape neck
Next row: K. 40 (43, 45, 48, 51), turn and leave remaining sts. on a spare needle. Work on these sts. only.
Next row: Bind off 6 sts., p. to end.
K. 1 row.
Next row: Bind off 4 (5, 5, 6, 6) sts., p. to end.
Bind off.
Return to remaining sts.

Moulin Rouge
modeled by Tula

With RS facing, bind off first 24 sts., rejoin yarn and k. to end.
P. 1 row.
Next row: Bind off 6 sts., k. to end.
P. 1 row.
Next row: Bind off 4 (5, 5, 6, 6) sts., k. to end.
Bind off.

LEFT FRONT
Using smaller size needles and thistle, cast on 57 (61, 63, 65, 69) sts.
Rib row 1: K. 1, * p. 1, k. 1, rep. from * to end.
Rib row 2: P. 1, * k. 1, p. 1, rep. from * to end.
Work in stripes as given for back, inc. 1 st. at center of last row on the **1st and 4th sizes only**: 58 (61, 63, 66, 69) sts.
Change to larger size needles.
Place motif from chart as follows:
Row 1: K. 18 (20, 19, 21, 24) camel, 40 (41, 44, 45, 45) fudge.
Continue in pat. from chart, shaping armhole as indicated, until row 183 (187, 187, 189, 189) has been completed.
Shape front neck
Next row: Bind off 13 sts., p. to end.
Dec. 1 st. at neck edge until 30 (32, 34, 36, 39) sts. remain.
Work 15 (10, 10, 13, 13) rows even.
Bind off.

RIGHT FRONT
Working from chart for right front, work as given for left front, reversing all shaping.

RIGHT SLEEVE
Using smaller size needles and thistle, cast on 63 (69, 69, 75, 75) sts.
Work in rib as given for back, working 2 rows thistle, 30 rows cream, 3 rows thistle and 2 rows black.
Inc. row: In black rib 6 (4, 4, 2, 2), M. 1, * rib 5 (6, 6, 7, 7), M. 1, rep. from * to last 7 (5, 5, 3, 3) sts., rib to end: 74 (80, 80, 86, 86) sts.
Change to larger size needles and camel.
Proceed in St. st., increasing 1 st. each end of 5th row and then every 4th row until there are 124 (130, 130, 136, 136) sts.
P. 1 row.
Place motif on sleeve as follows:
Next row: K. 72 (75, 75, 78, 78) camel, 4 black, 48 (51, 51, 54, 54) camel.
Increasing 1 st. each end of row 3, work in pat. from chart until row 12 has been completed: 126 (132, 132, 138, 138) sts.
Work 2 (6, 12, 14, 20) rows even in camel.
Bind off.

LEFT SLEEVE
Work as given for right sleeve until there are 108 (114, 114, 120, 120) sts.
P. 1 row.
Place motif on sleeve as follows:
Next row: K. 34 (37, 37, 40, 40) camel, 8 black, 4 camel, 3 black, 9 camel, 3 black, 6 camel, 8 black, 33 (36, 36, 39, 39) camel.
Increasing 1 st. each end of row 3 and then every 4th row, work in pat. from chart until there are 126 (132, 132, 138, 138) sts.
Work even from chart until row 40 has been completed.
Work 6 (10, 16, 18, 24) rows even in camel.
Bind off.

NECKBAND
Join shoulder seams.
With RS facing, using smaller size needles and black, pick up and k. 25 (26, 26, 27, 27) sts. up right front neck, 33 (35, 35, 37, 37) sts. across back neck and 25 (26, 26, 27, 27) sts. down left front neck; 83 (87, 87, 91, 91) sts.
With black, p. 1 row.
Working in rib as given for back, work 2 rows black, 3 rows thistle, 9 rows cream, 3 rows scarlet and 6 rows black.
Bind off in rib.
Fold neckband in half to WS and slipstitch into place.

(light gray)	Camel (018)
(white)	Cream (015)
(black)	Black (024)
(dark gray)	Thistle (123)
(gray)	Scarlet (012)
(gray)	Fudge (017)
(pale gray)	Daffodil (073)
/	Backstitch embroidery worked in Black (024)

BUTTONBAND

** With RS facing, using smaller size needles and cream, pick up and k. 149 (151, 155, 157, 159) sts. down left front. P. 1 row. **
Work 11 rows in rib as given for back. Change to thistle and rib 3 more rows. Bind off in rib.

TO MAKE UP

Block and press pieces lightly under a damp cloth following instructions on ball band.
Joining bound-off edges at armholes to underarms of sleeves, sew in sleeves, then join side and sleeve seams. Sew on buttons to correspond with buttonholes. Work embroidery in backstitch as indicated on chart. Sew in shoulder pads if required.

BUTTONHOLE BAND

Picking sts. up along right front, work as given for buttonband from ** to **.
Work 6 rows in rib.
Buttonhole row: Rib 4 (5, 5, 4, 5), bind off 6 sts., * rib 28 (28, 29, 30, 30) sts., bind off 6 sts., rep from * to last 3 (4, 4, 3, 4) sts., rib to end.
Next row: Rib to end, casting on 6 sts. over those bound off in previous row.
Now work 3 rows rib in white then 3 rows in thistle.
Bind off in rib.

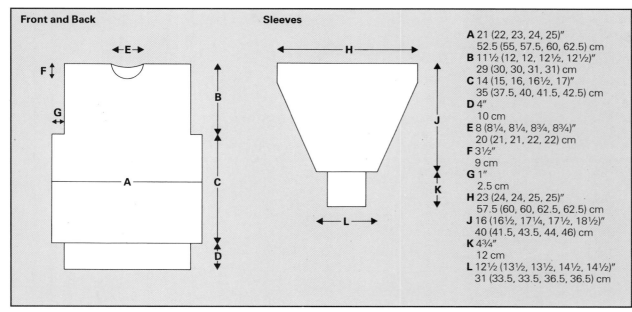

Front and Back

Sleeves

A 21 (22, 23, 24, 25)"
52.5 (55, 57.5, 60, 62.5) cm
B 11½ (12, 12, 12½, 12½)"
29 (30, 30, 31, 31) cm
C 14 (15, 16, 16½, 17)"
35 (37.5, 40, 41.5, 42.5) cm
D 4"
10 cm
E 8 (8¼, 8¼, 8¾, 8¾)"
20 (21, 21, 22, 22) cm
F 3½"
9 cm
G 1"
2.5 cm
H 23 (24, 24, 25, 25)"
57.5 (60, 60, 62.5, 62.5) cm
J 16 (16½, 17¼, 17½, 18½)"
40 (41.5, 43.5, 44, 46) cm
K 4¾"
12 cm
L 12½ (13½, 13½, 14½, 14½)"
31 (33.5, 33.5, 36.5, 36.5) cm

HENRI DE TOULOUSE-LAUTREC

Aristide Bruant at the Ambassadeurs

Aristide Bruant, with his distinctive hat, scarf and stick was a satirical cabaret singer. The manager of the Ambassadeurs club was outraged at this poster painted in 1892 as he felt the silhouette of the man leaning in the doorway evoked a sleazy atmosphere. Bruant threatened to cancel his appearance unless the poster was used.

The figure appears on the front of the garment. The back and sleeves are plain, just using the background colors of the poster. The cuffs are knitted in a contrasting color to complement those in the original.

SIZE
One size only to fit 32 to 40"/80 to 100cm chest

MATERIALS
Berger du Nord Douceur No. 4
6 × 50g balls in Yellow (shade 9172)
5 × 50g balls in Royal (shade 8540)
3 × 50g balls each in Navy (shade 8542) and Jade (shade 9189)
1 × 50g ball each in Écru (shade 8524), Black (shade 8521), Beige (shade 9170) and Orange (shade 8943)
A pair each of sizes 3 (3¼mm) and 6 (4mm) knitting needles.

GAUGE
22 sts. and 30 rows to 4"/10cm over St. st. worked on size 6 (4mm) needles.
Check your gauge

NOTES
When working motif, use separate, small balls of yarn. When joining in a new color, leave an end of about 2"/5cm for weaving in later, and when changing color, twist yarns together at back of work to avoid making a hole.

BACK
** Using smaller size needles and jade, cast on 137 sts.
Rib row 1: K. 1, * p. 1, k. 1, rep. from * to end.
Rib row 2: P. 1, * k. 1, p. 1, rep. from * to end.
Rep. these 2 rows for 2¼"/6cm, inc. 1 st. at center of last row: 138 sts. **

Aristide Bruant at
the Ambassadeurs
modeled by Mike
Read

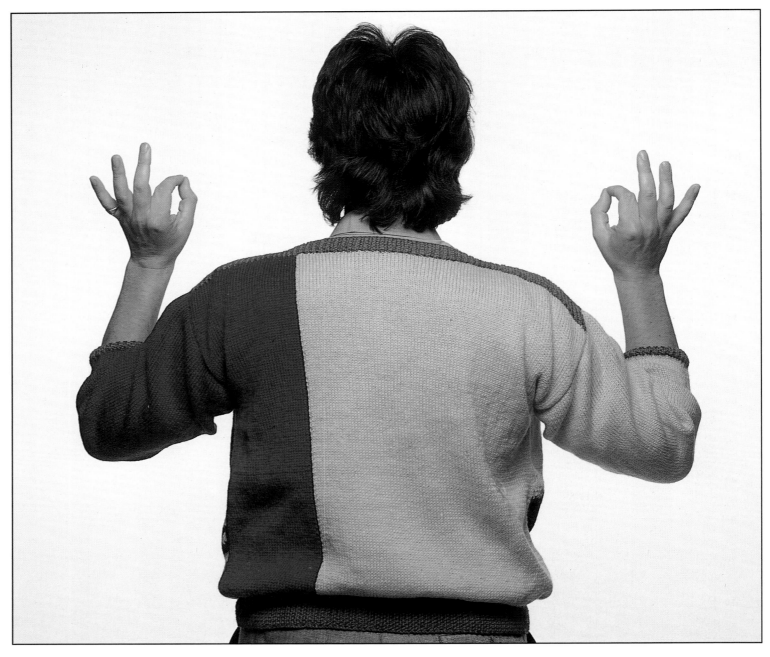

Change to larger size needles.
Work in 2-color pat. as follows:
Row 1: K. 94 yellow, 44 royal.
Row 2: P. 44 royal, 94 yellow.
Rep. these 2 rows until 151 rows have been completed.
Change to jade and p. 1 row.
Change to smaller size needles.
With jade work 10 rows k. 1, p. 1 rib.
Bind off in rib.

FRONT
Work as given for back from ** to **.
Change to larger size needles.
Place motif from chart as follows:
Row 1: K. 66 navy, 3 orange, 11 beige, 1

black, 11 beige, 46 navy.
Continue in pat. from chart until row 51 has been completed.
Change to jade and p. 1 row.
Now complete to match back.

RIGHT SLEEVE
Using smaller size needles and jade, cast on 63 sts.
Rep. the 2 rib rows as given for back for 1"/2.5cm inc. 1 st. at center of last row: 64 sts.
Change to larger needles and yellow.
Proceed in St. st. increasing 1 st. each end of first row and then every 4th row until there are 110 sts., ending with a k.

row.
Work 39 rows even.
Bind off.

LEFT SLEEVE
Work as given for right sleeve working cuff in jade and St. st. in royal.

TO MAKE UP
Block and press pieces lightly under a damp cloth following instructions on ball band.
Join shoulder seams leaving approximately 9"/23cm open for neck.
Sew in sleeves. Join side and sleeve seams.

Front

AMBASSADEURS

aristide BRUANT

	Yellow (9172)
	Royal (8540)
	Navy (8542)
	Écru (8524)
	Black (8521)
	Beige (9170)
	Orange (8943)

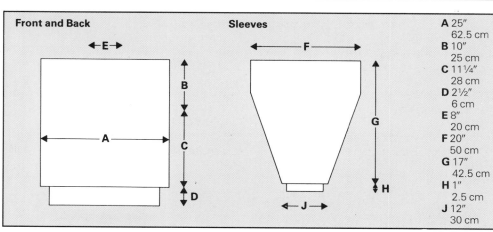

Front and Back   **Sleeves**

A	25″
	62.5 cm
B	10″
	25 cm
C	11¼″
	28 cm
D	2½″
	6 cm
E	8″
	20 cm
F	20″
	50 cm
G	17″
	42.5 cm
H	1″
	2.5 cm
J	12″
	30 cm

CLAUDE MONET
Water-lilies

M onet painted the water-lily pond at the bottom of his garden at Giverny hundreds of times; it became virtually his only "model" for the last twenty years of his life (1840–1926). The lilies themselves are not immediately recognizable, but dissolve instead into the delicate background colors.

Mohair is the only yarn in this cardigan, knitted in a neat forties style, because it shares the subtle shades and tones used by Monet in this wonderfully soft work. The lilies are knitted in plain white mohair in selected areas with the only sharp colors embroidered in red and yellow.

SIZES
To fit 32 (34, 36, 38)"/81 (86, 91, 96) cm chest

MATERIALS
Hayfield Lugano Fancy
4 × 50g balls Berne (shade 093008)
3 × 50g balls Lucerne (shade 093001)
2 × 50g balls Geneva (shade 093003)
Hayfield Lugano Plain
1 × 50g ball Mt. Blanc (shade 094060)
A small amount of tapestry or knitting wool in red and yellow for embroidery
A pair each of sizes 8 (5mm) and 10 (6mm) knitting needles
5 glass buttons
Stitch holders

GAUGE
18 sts. and 20 rows to 4"/10cm over St. st. worked on size 10 (6mm) needles.
Check your gauge

NOTES
Instructions for the larger sizes are given in parentheses ( ).
When working motif, use separate, small balls of yarn. When joining in a new color, leave an end of about 2"/5cm for weaving in later, and when changing color, twist yarns together at back of work to avoid making a hole.

BACK
Using smaller size needles and berne, cast on 79 (83, 87, 91) sts.
Rib row 1: K. 1, * p. 1, k. 1, rep. from * to end.
Rib row 2: P. 1, * k. 1, p. 1, rep. from * to end.
Rep. these 2 rows for 2¼"/6cm, ending rib row 1.
Inc. row: Rib 14 (13, 14, 16), M. 1, * rib 13 (14, 15, 15), M. 1, rep. from * to last 13 (14, 13, 15) sts., rib to end: 84 (88, 92, 96) sts.
Change to larger size needles.
Beg. row 9 (7, 5, 1), work in pat. from chart, shaping armholes as indicated, until row 86 (90, 90, 92) is complete.
Shape neck
Next row: K. 29 (32, 34, 37), turn and leave remaining sts. on a spare needle. Work on these sts. only.
Next row: Bind off 4 (5, 5, 6) sts., p. to end.
K. 1 row.
Next row: Bind off 5 sts., p. to end.
Bind off.
Return to remaining sts.
With RS facing, slip first 12 sts. to a holder, rejoin yarn to next st. and k. to end.
P. 1 row.
Next row: Bind off 4 (5, 5, 6) sts., k. to end.

Water-lilies modeled by Jane Asher

P. 1 row.
Next row: Bind off 5 sts., k. to end.
Bind off.

LEFT FRONT

Using smaller size needles and berne, cast on 39 (41, 43, 45) sts.
Work 2¼"/6cm in rib as given for back, ending rib row 1.
Inc. row: Rib 9 (10, 10, 11), M. 1, * rib 10 (10, 11, 11), M. 1, rep. from * to last 10 (11, 11, 12) sts., rib to end; 42 (44, 46, 48) sts.
Change to larger size needles.
Beg. row 9 (7, 5, 1), work in pat. from chart, shaping armhole as indicated, until row 75 (79, 79, 81) has been completed.

Shape neck
Continuing in pat. following chart, bind off 7 sts. at beg. of next row.
Dec. 1 st. at neck edge on every row until 21 (28, 30, 35) sts. remain.
Next row: Dec. 1 st. at neck edge and inc. 1 st. at armhole edge.
Continue dec. 1 st. at neck edge only until 20 (22, 24, 26) sts. remain.
Work 7 (6, 6, 5) rows even.
Bind off.

RIGHT FRONT

Working from chart for right front, work as given for left front, reversing shaping.

LEFT SLEEVE

Using smaller size needles and berne, cast on 51 (53, 53, 55) sts.
Work 3½"/9cm in rib as given for back, ending rib row 1.
Inc. row: Rib 9 (8, 8, 9), M. 1, * rib 8 (9, 9, 9), M. 1, rep. from * to last 10 (9, 9, 10) sts., rib to end: 56 (58, 58, 60) sts.
Change to larger size needles.
Beg. at row 9 (5, 3, 1), work in pat. from chart, shaping sleeve as indicated by inc. 1 st. each end of 5th row and then every 4th row until there are 76 (78, 78, 80) sts. and row 70 has been completed.

Shape sleeve cap
Continuing in pat. following chart, bind off 3 sts. at beg. of every row until 28 (36, 36, 44) sts. remain, then bind off 4 sts. at beg. of every row until 12 sts. remain.
Bind off.

RIGHT SLEEVE

Working from chart for right sleeve, work as given for left sleeve.

NECKBAND

Join shoulder seams.
With RS facing, using smaller size

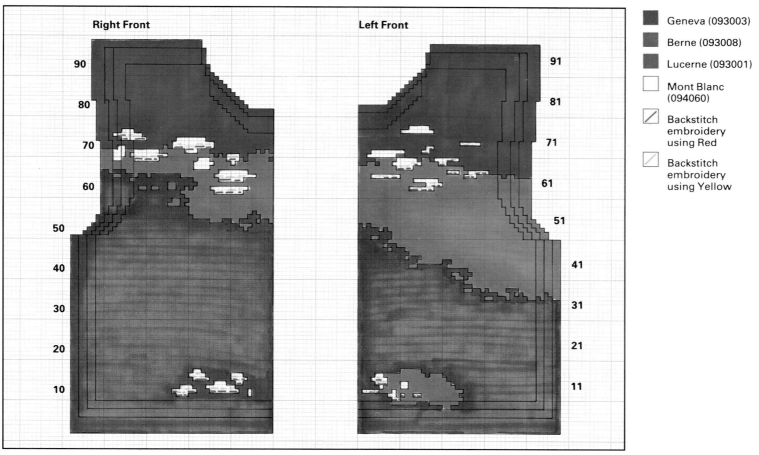

Right Front

Left Front

Geneva (093003)

Berne (093008)

Lucerne (093001)

Mont Blanc
(094060)

Backstitch
embroidery
using Red

Backstitch
embroidery
using Yellow

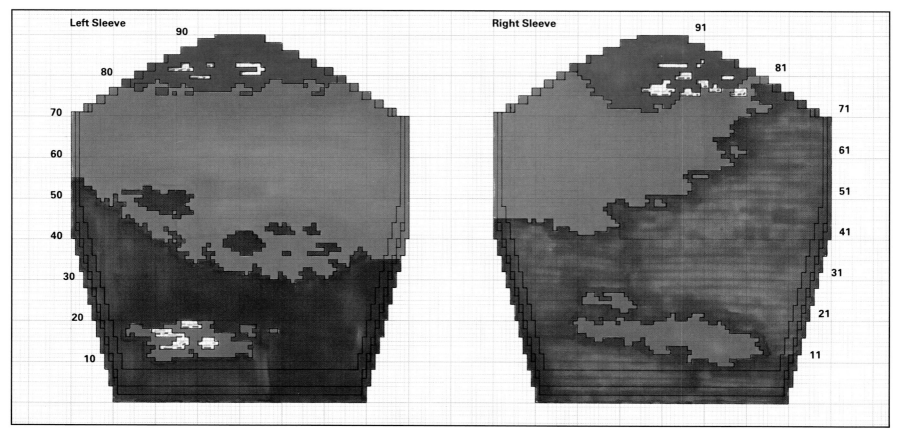

Left Sleeve

Right Sleeve

needles and geneva, pick up and k. 20 (21, 21, 22) sts. up right front neck, 10 (11, 11, 12) down right back neck, k. across 12 sts. from holder, pick up and k. 11 (12, 12, 13) sts. up left back neck and 20 (21, 21, 22) sts. down left front neck: 73 (77, 77, 81) sts.
Work 4 rows in rib as given for back.
Bind off in rib.

BUTTONBAND
Using smaller size needles and berne, cast on 7 sts.
Work 56 (58, 60, 62) rows in rib as given for back, then work 16 rows in lucerne, and 14 (16, 16, 18) rows in geneva.
Bind off in rib.

BUTTONHOLE BAND
Using smaller size needles and berne, cast on 7 sts.
Work 4 (4, 6, 6) rows rib.
Next row: Rib 3, bind off 1 st., rib to end.
Next row: Rib 3, cast on 1 st., rib to end. These last 2 rows form the buttonhole.
* Rib 17 (18, 18, 19) rows.
Work the 2 buttonhole rows.
Rep. from * once more.
Work 12 rows in berne, then 5 (6, 6, 7)

rows in lucerne.
Work the 2 buttonhole rows, then rib 9 (8, 8, 7) rows.
Change to geneva and rib 8 (10, 10, 12) more rows.
Work the 2 buttonhole rows once more.
Rib 4 rows.
Bind off in rib.

TO MAKE UP
Block and press pieces lightly under a damp cloth following instructions on ball band. Work in buttonhole st. round each buttonhole to strengthen. Work embroidery in backstitch as indicated on chart. Sew buttonband to left front and buttonhole band to right front; sew on buttons to correspond with buttonholes. Sew in sleeves, then join side and sleeve seams.

SHOULDER PADS (Make 2)
Using larger size needles and geneva, cast on 20 sts.
Work 28 rows in garter st.
Bind off.
Fold each piece diagonally in half. Sew edges together. Sew shoulder pads in place, placing folded edge at armhole seam.

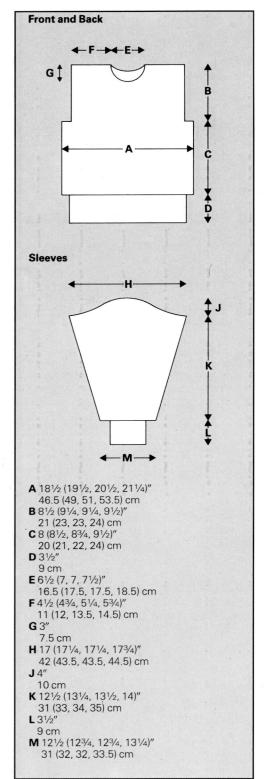

Front and Back

Sleeves

A 18½ (19½, 20½, 21¼)"
46.5 (49, 51, 53.5) cm
B 8½ (9¼, 9¼, 9½)"
21 (23, 23, 24) cm
C 8 (8½, 8¾, 9½)"
20 (21, 22, 24) cm
D 3½"
9 cm
E 6½ (7, 7, 7½)"
16.5 (17.5, 17.5, 18.5) cm
F 4½ (4¾, 5¼, 5¾)"
11 (12, 13.5, 14.5) cm
G 3"
7.5 cm
H 17 (17¼, 17¼, 17¾)"
42 (43.5, 43.5, 44.5) cm
J 4"
10 cm
K 12½ (13¼, 13½, 14)"
31 (33, 34, 35) cm
L 3½"
9 cm
M 12½ (12¾, 12¾, 13¼)"
31 (32, 32, 33.5) cm

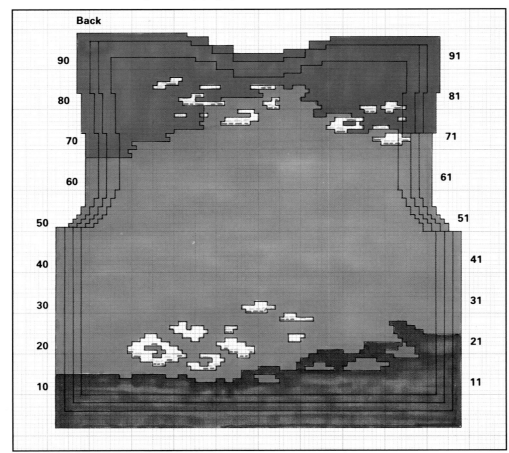

Back

PIET MONDRIAN
Square Composition

In his most famous works, Mondrian (1892–1944) used only black and white plus the three primary colors. This geometric work with its straight lines and colored rectangles could not be further removed from the landscape paintings of his early career.

In the 1960s, Yves St. Laurent styled a dress around one of these abstracts. It was this that inspired the sweater.

SIZES
To fit 36 (38, 40, 42, 44, 46)"/90 (95, 100, 105, 110, 115) cm chest

MATERIALS
Scheepjeswool Mayflower Cotton Helarsgarn
Crew Neck
13 (14, 14, 15, 15, 16) × 50g balls in White (shade 902)
Polo neck
14 (14, 15, 15, 16, 16) × 50g balls in White (shade 902)
Both sweaters
1 × 50g ball each in Yellow (shade 908), Black (shade 915), Red (shade 910) and Blue (shade 906)

A pair each of sizes 6 (4mm) and 7 (4½mm) knitting needles
Raglan shoulder pads (optional)
Stitch holders

GAUGE
18 sts. and 25 rows to 4"/10cm over St. st. worked on size 7 (4½mm) needles.
Check your gauge

NOTES
Instructions for the larger sizes are given in parentheses ( ).
When working motif, use separate, small balls of yarn. When joining in a new color, leave an end of about 2"/5cm for weaving in later. When changing color, twist yarns together at back of work to avoid making a hole.

BACK
Using smaller size needles and white, cast on 93 (97, 103, 107, 111, 115) sts.
Row 1: * K. 1, p. 1, rep. from * to last st., k. 1.
Row 2: * P. 1, k. 1, rep. from * to last st., p. 1.
Rep. these 2 rows for 2¾"/7cm, ending with row 2.

Change to larger needles and work 72 (74, 76, 80, 84, 86) rows St. st.
Shape raglans
Dec. 1 st. each end of next 8 (8, 10, 10, 12, 14) rows.
Next row: (RS) K. 3, k. 2 tog. tbl., k. to last 5 sts., k. 2 tog., k. 3.
Work 2 rows.
Next row: (WS) P. 3, p. 2 tog., p. to last 5 sts., p. 2 tog. tbl., p. 3.
Work 2 rows.
Rep. these 6 rows until 39 (41, 43, 47, 47, 47) sts. remain.
Shape back neck
1st size only
P. 1 row.
4th, 5th and 6th sizes only
P. 1 row.
K. 1 row. Dec. 1 st. each end of next row.
All sizes
K. 13 (14, 15, 16, 16, 16) sts., turn and leave remaining sts. on a spare needle.
Work on these sts. only.
Bind off 5 (5, 6, 6, 6, 6) sts., p. to last 5 sts., p. 2 tog. tbl., p. 3.
K. 1 row.
Next row: Bind off 5 (6, 6, 7, 7, 7) sts., p. to end.

Square
Composition
modeled by
Julianne White

K. 2 tog., then break yarn and pull through last stitch.
Return to remaining sts.
With RS facing, slip first 13 sts. to a holder.
Join on yarn and k. to end.
Next row: P. 3, p. 2 tog., p. to end.
Next row: Bind off 5 (5, 6, 6, 6, 6) sts., k. to end.
Next row: P. 3, p. 2 tog., p. to end.
Bind off remaining 6 (7, 7, 8, 8, 8) sts.

FRONT
Work as given for back until 14 (16, 18, 22, 26, 28) rows of St. st. have been worked.

Place motif as follows:
Row 1: K. 46 (48, 51, 53, 55, 57) white, join in black, k. 1 black, k. 46 (48, 51, 53, 55, 57) white.
Row 2: P. 45 (47, 50, 52, 54, 56) white, p. 3 black, join in 2nd ball of white, p. 45 (47, 50, 52, 54, 56) white.
Continue working from chart, and *at the same time* when row 58 of chart has been completed work raglan shaping as given for back until 51 (53, 55, 59, 59, 59) sts. remain.
First size only
P. 1 row.

4th, 5th and 6th sizes only
K. 1 row, then p. 1 row.
Shape front neck
1st, 2nd and 3rd sizes only
K. 20 (21, 22), turn and leave remaining sts. on a holder.
4th, 5th and 6th sizes only
K. 3, k. 2 tog. tbl., k. 19, turn and leave remaining sts. on a holder.
All sizes
Continue shaping raglan edge as before, at the same time dec. 1 st. at neck edge on every row until 5 sts. remain.
1st size only
K. 1 row.
2nd size only
P. 1 row.
1st, 2nd and 3rd sizes only
Dec. 1 st. at raglan edge on next row and then every 3rd row 2 (1, 1) times.
Work 1 row.
All sizes
Dec. 1 st. at raglan edge every other row 2 (3, 3, 4, 4, 4) times.
Break yarn and pull through last st.
Return to remaining sts.
With RS facing, slip first 11 sts. to a holder, rejoin yarn and work 2nd side of neck to match first, reversing all shaping.

SLEEVES
Using smaller size needles and white, cast on 45 (47, 47, 51, 51, 53) sts.
Work rib as given for back for 26 rows.
Inc. row: Rib 9 (10, 10, 11, 11, 12), M. 1, * rib 9 (9, 9, 10, 10, 10), M. 1, rep. from * to last 9 (10, 10, 10, 10, 11) sts., rib to end: 49 (51, 51, 55, 55, 57) sts.
Change to larger needles and working in St. st., inc. 1 st. each end of 5th row and then every 6th row until there are 73 (77, 77, 81, 81, 85) sts.
Work 23 (21, 25, 27, 29, 31) rows even.
Shape raglan
Dec. 1 st. each end of next 6 (8, 7, 9, 8, 10) rows, then at each end of every 3rd row until 33 sts. remain.
Work 2 rows.
Next row: K. 2 tog. tbl., k. 13, sl. 1, k. 2 tog., psso., k. 13, k. 2 tog.
Continue to work raglan shaping as before, at the same time shape shoulder by working sl. 1, k. 2 tog., psso. at center of every RS row 7 times more: 7 sts.
Continue shaping at raglan edge only until 5 sts. remain.
Work 2 rows. Leave sts. on a holder.
Join front and left back raglan seams.

NECKBAND
Using smaller size needles and white, and with RS facing, pick up and k. 7 (7, 9,

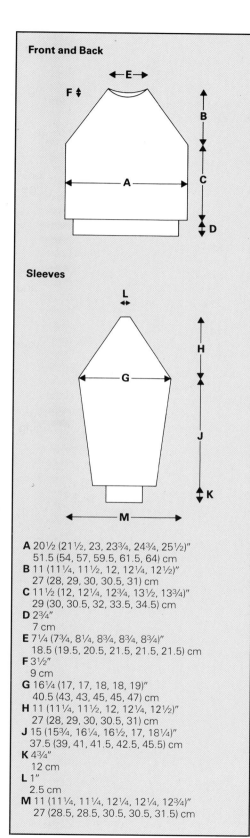

Front and Back

Sleeves

A 20½ (21½, 23, 23¾, 24¾, 25½)"
   51.5 (54, 57, 59.5, 61.5, 64) cm
B 11 (11¼, 11½, 12, 12¼, 12½)"
   27 (28, 29, 30, 30.5, 31) cm
C 11½ (12, 12¼, 12¾, 13½, 13¾)"
   29 (30, 30.5, 32, 33.5, 34.5) cm
D 2¾"
   7 cm
E 7¼ (7¾, 8¼, 8¾, 8¾, 8¾)"
   18.5 (19.5, 20.5, 21.5, 21.5, 21.5) cm
F 3½"
   9 cm
G 16¼ (17, 17, 18, 18, 19)"
   40.5 (43, 43, 45, 45, 47) cm
H 11 (11¼, 11½, 12, 12¼, 12½)"
   27 (28, 29, 30, 30.5, 31) cm
J 15 (15¾, 16¼, 16½, 17, 18¼)"
   37.5 (39, 41, 41.5, 42.5, 45.5) cm
K 4¾"
   12 cm
L 1"
   2.5 cm
M 11 (11¼, 11¼, 12¼, 12¼, 12¾)"
   27 (28.5, 28.5, 30.5, 30.5, 31.5) cm

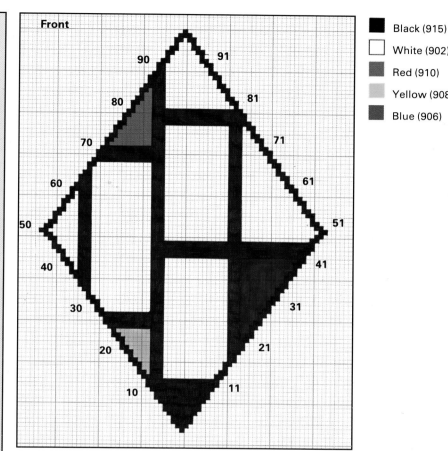

Front

Black (915)
White (902)
Red (910)
Yellow (908)
Blue (906)

11, 11, 11) sts. down right back neck, k.
across 13 sts. of center back neck, pick
up and k. 8 (8, 10, 12, 12, 12) sts. up left
back neck, k. across 5 sts. at top of
sleeve, pick up and k. 23 (23, 23, 25, 25,
25) sts. down left front neck, k. across 11
sts. of center front neck, pick up and k.
23 (23, 23, 25, 25, 25) sts. up right front
neck, then k. across 5 sts. at top of right
sleeves: 95 (95, 99, 107, 107, 107) sts.
P. 1 row.
Work 10 rows of k. 1, p. 1 rib for crew
neck or 30 rows of k. 1, p. 1 rib for turtle
neck.
Bind off loosely in rib.

TO MAKE UP
Block and press pieces lightly under a
damp cloth following instructions on ball
band.
Join right back raglan and neckband
seam.
For crew neck, fold rib in half to wrong
side and slipstitch bound-off edge into
position.
Join side and sleeve seams.
Sew in shoulder pads if required.

PIET MONDRIAN
Red, Yellow and Blue

This is from one of Mondrian's more complicated geometrical works created between 1939 and 1942. Again, he uses flat planes of color with grids of black and white.
A rather severe shape was chosen for this sweater which has straight padded shoulders with set-in sleeves. The painting is repeated on the back of the garment giving a sense of continuity.

SIZES
One size only to fit 32 to 40"/80 to 100cm chest

MATERIALS
Scheepjeswool Mayflower Cotton Helarsgarn
16 × 50g balls in White (shade 902)
4 × 50g balls in Black (shade 915)
1 × 50g ball each in Yellow (shade 908), Red (shade 910) and Blue (shade 906)
A pair each of sizes 6 (4mm) and 7 (4½mm) knitting needles
One size 6 (4mm) circular knitting needle
One 6"/15cm zipper
Large shoulder pads; Stitch holder

GAUGE
18 sts. and 25 rows to 4"/10cm over St. st. worked on size 7 (4½mm) needles.
Check your gauge

NOTES
When working motifs, use separate, small balls of yarn. When joining in a new color, leave an end of about 2"/5cm for weaving in later, and when changing color, twist yarns together at back of work to avoid making a hole.

BACK
Using smaller size needles and white, cast on 97 sts.
Rib row 1: K. 1, * p. 1, k. 1, rep. from * to end.
Rib row 2: P. 1, * k. 1, p. 1, rep. from * to end.
Rep. these 2 rows 7 times more, then work rib row 1 again.
Inc. row: * Rib 24, M. 1, rep. from * to last 25 sts., rib to end: 100 sts.
Change to larger size needles and work from chart until row 92 has been completed.

Shape armholes
Dec. 1 st. each end of every row until 84 sts. remain.
Continue working from chart until row 144 has been completed.
Shape back neck
Continuing in pat. following chart, k. 32, turn and leave remaining sts. on a spare needle.
Work on these sts. only.
Next row: Bind off 6 sts., p. to end.
K. 1 row.
Next row: Bind off 4 sts., p. to end.
Bind off.
Return to remaining sts.
With RS facing, slip first 20 sts. to a holder.
Rejoin yarn and k. to end.
P. 1 row.
Next row: Bind off 6 sts., k. to end.
P. 1 row.
Next row: Bind off 4 sts., k. to end.
Bind off.

FRONT
Work as given for back until row 104 of chart has been completed.

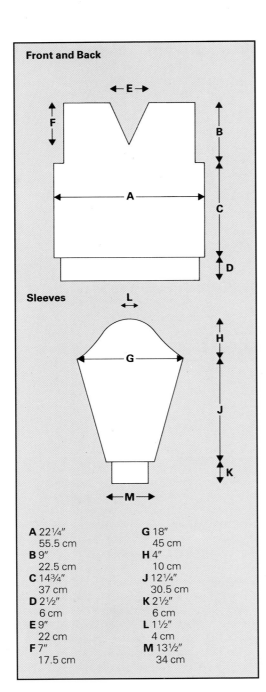

Front and Back

Sleeves

A 22¼"	**G** 18"
55.5 cm	45 cm
B 9"	**H** 4"
22.5 cm	10 cm
C 14¾"	**J** 12¼"
37 cm	30.5 cm
D 2½"	**K** 2½"
6 cm	6 cm
E 9"	**L** 1½"
22 cm	4 cm
F 7"	**M** 13½"
17.5 cm	34 cm

Shape front neck
Continuing in pat. following chart, k. 42 sts., turn and leave remaining sts. on a spare needle.
Work on these sts. only.
Dec. 1 st. at neck edge every other row until 22 sts. remain.
Work even until row 148 has been completed.
Bind off.
Return to remaining sts.
With RS facing, rejoin yarn at center front and work to end.
Work 2nd side of neck to match first, reversing all shaping.

SLEEVES
Using smaller size needles and white, cast on 51 sts.
Rep. the 2 rib rows of back for 2¼"/6cm, ending rib row 1.
Inc. row: Rib 3, M. 1, * rib 5, M. 1, rep. from * to last 3 sts., rib to end: 61 sts.
Change to larger size needles and work in St. st., increasing 1 st. each end of 5th row and then every 4th row until there are 77 sts.
P. 1 row.
Increasing 1 st. at each end of 3rd row, work 3 rows in black.
Increasing 1 st. at each end of 4th row, work 22 rows in white: 81 sts.
Keep working even, work 3 rows black, 13 rows white and 1 row black.

Shape sleeve
Still using black, dec. 1 st., each end of next 2 rows.
Using white, dec. 1 st. each end of next 10 rows: 57 sts.
Using black, bind off 3 sts. at beg. of next 3 rows, then using white bind off 3 sts. at beg. of next 3 rows: 39 sts.
Using white, bind off 3 sts., then k. 14, sl. 1, k. 2 tog., psso., k. 18.
Next row: Bind off 3 sts., p. to end.
Continuing to bind off 3 sts. at beg. of every row, shape sleeve cap by working sl. 1, k. 2 tog., psso. at center of every RS row until 7 sts. remain.
Bind off.

COLLAR
Join shoulder seams.
Using circular needle and white and with RS facing, pick up and k. 46 sts. up right side of neck, 9 sts. down right back neck, k. across 20 sts. at center back, pick up and k. 10 sts. up left back neck and 46 sts. down left front neck: 131 sts.
P. 1 row. Working back and forth as with straight needles, work 2 rows in rib as given for back.

Next row: K. 1, p. 1, sl. 1, k. 2 tog. tbl., psso., rib 39, sl. 1, k. 2 tog. tbl., psso., rib 37, k. 3 tog., rib to last 5 sts., k. 3 tog., p. 1, k. 1.
Next row: P. 1, * k. 1, p. 1, rep. from * to end.
Next row: K. 1, p. 1, sl. 1, k. 2 tog. tbl., psso., rib 34, p. 3 tog. tbl., k. 1, p. 3 tog., rib 31, p. 3 tog. tbl., k. 1, p. 3 tog., rib to last 5 sts., k. 3 tog., p. 1, k. 1.
Next row: P. 1, * k. 1, p. 1, rep. from * to end.
Next row: K. 1, p. 1, sl. 1, k. 2 tog. tbl., psso., rib 30, p. 3 tog. tbl., k. 1, p. 3 tog., rib 27, p. 3 tog. tbl., k. 1, p. 3 tog., rib to last 5 sts., k. 3 tog., p. 1, k. 1.

Continue working in rib, working decreases as before *at center front edges only* until 63 sts. remain.
Rib 1 row.
Bind off in rib.

TO MAKE UP
Block and press pieces lightly under a damp cloth following instructions on ball band.
Join side seams, matching horizontal lines.
Join sleeve seams and set in sleeves, matching lines at armholes. Sew in zipper. Sew in shoulder pads.

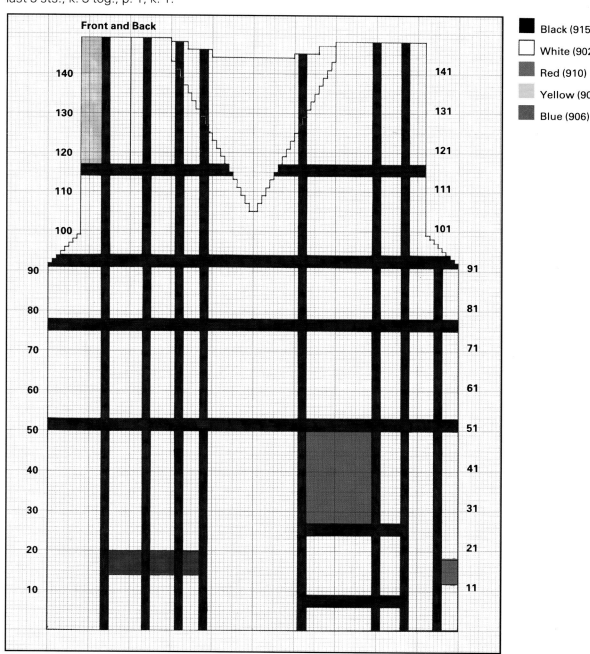

Front and Back

| Black (915) |
| White (902) |
| Red (910) |
| Yellow (908) |
| Blue (906) |

ROY LICHTENSTEIN

Whaam

One frame taken from a comic strip makes this American pop-art classic of 1963. A characteristic image of the 1960s, this just had to be knitted! A fine cotton has been chosen to produce as much detail as possible. The natural division in the painting has been used imaginatively to design the back and front, and as a result there is a marked contrast in the look of the two different sides of the sweater.

SIZES
One size only to fit 32 to 40"/80 to 100cm chest

MATERIALS
Pingouin coton Naturel 8 Fils
8 × 50g balls Azur (shade 99)
3 × 50g balls each of Blanc (shade 80) and Soleil (shade 82)
2 × 50g balls each of Noir (shade 104) and Corrida (shade 84)
1 × 50g ball Plomb (shade 101)
A pair each of sizes 3 (3¼mm) and 6 (4mm) knitting needles
Stitch holders

GAUGE
20 sts. and 26 rows to 4"/10cm over St. st. worked on size 6 (4mm) needles.
Check your gauge

NOTES
When working motif, use separate, small balls of yarn. When joining in a new color, leave an end of about 2"/5cm for weaving in later, and when changing color, twist yarns together at back of work to avoid making a hole.

BACK
** Using smaller size needles and azur, cast on 119 sts.
Rib row 1: K. 1, * p. 1, k. 1, rep. from * to end.
Rib row 2: P. 1, * k. 1, p. 1, rep. from * to end.
Rep. these 2 rows for 3"/7½cm, ending with rib row 2 and increasing 1 st. at end of last row: 120 sts. **
Change to larger size needles.
Work in pat. from chart for back as follows:
Row 1: K. 4 azur, 6 blanc, 5 corrida, 13 azur, 6 corrida, 1 noir, 5 blanc, 36 corrida,

ROY LICHTENSTEIN

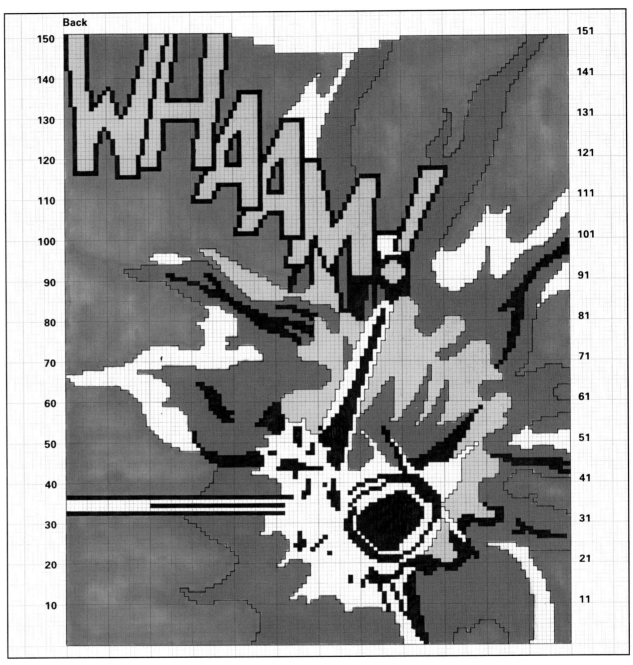

Legend:
- Azur (99)
- Blanc (80)
- Soleil (82)
- Noir (104)
- Corrida (84)
- Plomb (101)

44 azur.
Continue in pat. as established until row 146 has been completed.
Shape neck
Next row: Continuing in pat. following chart, k. 50, turn and leave remaining sts. on a spare needle.
Next row: Bind off 5 sts., p. to end.
K. 1 row.
Next row: Bind off 5 sts., p. to end.
Bind off.
Return to remaining sts.
With RS facing, slip first 20 sts. to a holder, join yarn to next st. and k. to end.
P. 1 row.

Next row: Bind off 5 sts., k. to end.
P. 1 row.
Next row: Bind off 5 sts., k. to end.
Bind off.

FRONT
Work as given for back from ** to **
Change to larger size needles.
Work in pat. from chart for front as follows:
Row 1: K. 1 azur, 1 noir, 34 blanc, 1 noir, 83 azur.
Continue in pat. as established until row 134 has been completed.
Shape neck

Next row: K. 50, turn and leave remaining sts. on a spare needle.
Dec. 1 st. at neck edge every row until 40 sts. remain.
Work 5 rows even.
Bind off.
Return to remaining sts.
With RS facing, slip first 20 sts. to a holder, join yarn to next st., then keeping pat. as established work 2nd side of neck to match first, reversing all shaping.

LEFT SLEEVE
Using smaller size needles and azur, cast on 55 sts.

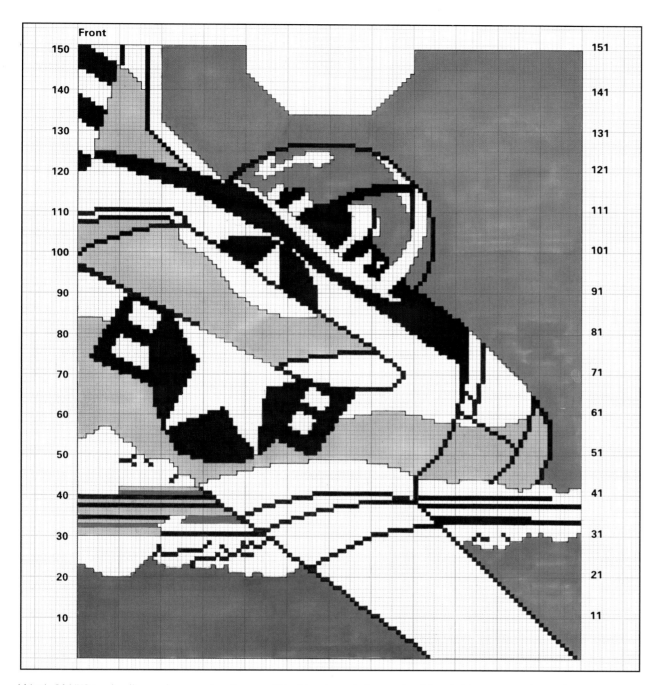

Work 2¼"/6cm in rib as given on back, ending with rib row 1.
Inc. row: Rib 15, M. 1, * rib 13, M. 1, rep. from * to last 14 sts. rib to end: 58 sts.
Change to larger size needles.
Work in St. st. increasing 1 st. each end of 5th row and then every 4th row until there are 100 sts. Work 19 rows even. Bind off.

RIGHT SLEEVE
Work cuff as given for left sleeve to end of increase row: 58 sts.
Change to larger size needles.

Working in pat. from chart for right sleeve, complete to match left sleeve.

NECKBAND
Join left shoulder seam.
With RS facing and using smaller size needles and azur, pick up and k. 15 sts. down right side of back neck, k. across 20 sts. from holder, pick up and k. 16 sts. up left side of back neck and 17 sts. down left side of front neck, k. across 20 sts. from holder, then pick up and k. 17 sts. up right side of front neck: 105 sts. P. 1 row.
Rib row 1: K. 1, * p. 1, k. 1, rep. from *

to end.
Rib row 2: P. 1, * k. 1, p. 1, rep. from * to end.
Rep. these 2 rows once more.
Bind off in rib.

TO MAKE UP
Block and press pieces lightly under a damp cloth following instructions on ball band.
Join right shoulder and neckband seam.
Sew in sleeves. Join side and sleeve seams.

ROY LICHTENSTEIN

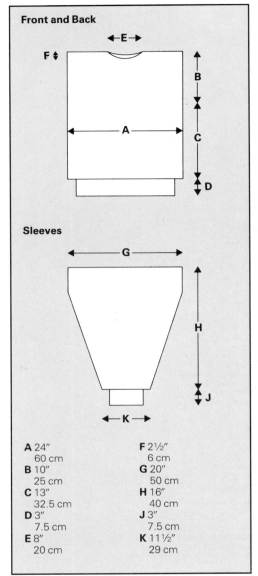

Front and Back

F ↕

E

A

B

C

D

Sleeves

G

H

J

K

A	24″	**F**	2½″
	60 cm		6 cm
B	10″	**G**	20″
	25 cm		50 cm
C	13″	**H**	16″
	32.5 cm		40 cm
D	3″	**J**	3″
	7.5 cm		7.5 cm
E	8″	**K**	11½″
	20 cm		29 cm

Right Sleeve

I PRESSED THE FIRE
CONTROL... AND
AHEAD OF ME
ROCKETS BLAZED
THROUGH
THE SKY...

YARN SUPPLIERS

All the yarns in this book should be readily obtainable from good yarn suppliers. If you experience difficulty in finding a particular yarn please contact the relevant supplier directly at the address given below.

SUPPLIER	USA	CANADA
ANNY BLATT	Anny Blatt 24770 Crestview Court Farmington Hills, MI 48018	Anny Blatt Diamond Yarns Inc 9697 St Laurence Boulevard Montreal, PQ H3L 2N1
BERGER DU NORD	Berger du Nord 12075 NW 39th Street Cari Springs, FL 33065	Berger du Nord Diamond Yarns Inc 9697 St Laurence Boulevard Montreal, PQ H3L 2N1
BRUNSWICK	Brunswick Yarns PO Box 276 Pickens, SC 29671	S R Kertzer 257 Adelaide Street West Toronto, ON M5H 1Y1
HAYFIELD	Hayfield/Shepherd Wools Inc 711 Johnson Avenue Blaine, WA 98230	Hayfield/Craftsmen Distributors PO Box 374 Abbotsford, BC V2S 4N9
PATONS	Patons/Susan Bates Route 9A Chester, CT 06412	Patons & Baldwins Canada Inc 1001 Roselawn Avenue Toronto, ON M6B 1B8
PINGOUIN	Pingouin PO Box 100, Highway 45 Jamestown. SC 29453	Promafil Canada Limitée 1500 Jules Poitras St Laurent, PQ H4N 1X7
ROWAN	Rowan Yarns Westminster Trading Corporation 5 Northern Boulevard Amherst, NH 03031	Rowan Yarns Westminster Trading Corporation Estelle Design and Sales 38 Continental Place Scarborough, ON M1R 2T4
SCHAFFHAUSER	Schaffhauser 3489 NW Yeon Avenue (Building 3) Portland, OR 97210	White Knitting Products 1470 Birchmount Road Scarborough, ON M1P 2G1
SCHEEPJESWOOL	Scheepjeswool USA 199 Trade Zone Drive Ronkonkoma, NY 11779	Scheepjeswool (Canada) Ltd 400 B Montée de Liesse Montreal, PQ H4T 1N8

KNITTING KNOW-HOW

ABBREVIATIONS

k.	knit
p.	purl
st(s).	stitch(es)
St.st.	stockinette stitch
rev.St.st.	reversed stockinette stitch
pat.	pattern
rep.	repeat
beg.	beginning
inc.	increase(ing)
dec.	decrease(ing
tog.	together
sl.	slip
in.	inch(es)
mm	millimeters
cm	centimeters
psso.	pass slip stitch over
M. 1	make one
RS	right side
WS	wrong side
tbl.	through back of loop

READING CHARTS

The patterns in this book all use charts. Each chart consists of a grid, sometimes the entire piece being knitted into the actual shape marked up in the squares. Each square represents one stitch and each horizontal line of squares represents one row.

Unless otherwise given in the instructions the design as shown on the chart is worked in stockinette stitch, all odd numbered rows being read from right to left and worked as knit stitches (right-side rows) and all even numbered rows being read from left to right and worked as purl stitches (wrong-side rows).

Each square shows which color yarn is to be used for that stitch.

If on the design you are working there is only a small motif to be worked, then the chart is only given for that area of the sweater and the instructions will tell you where to place the motif within the row. All stitches either side of the chart are then worked in the main color.

If the chart is for the full section of the piece you are knitting, then it will usually indicate any shaping that needs to be done. If the number of squares varies at the side, armhole and neck edges, then increase or decrease that number of stitches at that point on the row you are working.

At the center front neck, where there are usually quite a few stitches to be shaped, either leave the center stitches on a holder or refer to the pattern instructions to see if it tells you to bind them off.

CHANGING COLORS

When working from the chart it is necessary to use several different colors, very often within the same row. If there are very small areas to be worked in any of the colors, then wind off a small amount of yarn either into a small ball or onto a bobbin. This will make working with a lot of colors easier and help keep them from getting tangled. When joining in a new color at the beginning of a row, insert the needle into the first stitch, make a loop in the new yarn, leaving an end to be later woven in, then place this loop over the needle and complete the stitch.

When joining in a new color in the middle of a row, work in the first color to the point where the new color is needed, then insert the needle into the next stitch and complete with the new color in the same way as for joining in at the beginning of a row.

When changing color along a row always make sure that the color that is being used is twisted around the next color to be used, otherwise the two stitches will not be linked together and a hole will form between them.

Changing Color

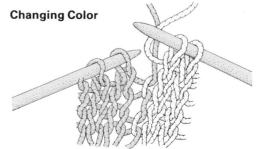

FINISHING

After knitting all the pieces for the garment, first weave in all the ends securely, then for a better finished look block all the pieces.

Firstly cover a large area with a thick blanket and a piece of clean fabric such as a sheet.

Lay out each piece of the garment and pin out to shape taking care not to stretch ribbing.

If the yarn can be pressed then cover with a damp cloth and press each piece lightly avoiding all ribbing. Do not move the iron over the fabric, but keep picking up and placing it lightly down again.

If the yarn cannot be pressed then cover with a damp cloth and leave until completely dry.

EMBROIDERY

Some of the designs have added embroidery to give extra detail. The first of these is called Backstitch and this is used whenever a line is needed. The second stitch used is a French Knot and this is used whenever spots or dots are needed.

Backstitch

Thread the needle with the required color of yarn and fasten at the back of the work. Bring the needle through to the right side of the fabric.

Backstitch

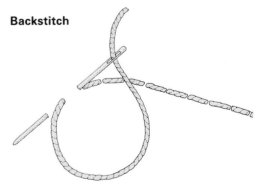

Insert the needle back through the fabric about ¼"/5mm to the right of where the yarn was brought through and then bring it back out again about ¼"/5mm to the left of the first stitch. Draw the needle

through, pulling the yarn gently.
Now insert the needle back into the
fabric at the end of the first stitch and
bring it out again ¼"/5mm further along.
Continue in this way until the line has
been completed, then fasten off
securely.

French Knots
Thread the needle with the required
color yarn and fasten at the back of the
work.
Bring the needle through to the right side
of the fabric at the position for the knot.
Take a small stitch of the fabric and wind
the yarn 2, 3 or 4 times round the point of
the needle (depending on how large the
knot is to be).
Pull the needle carefully through, then
insert the needle back through the fabric
at the base of the knot and fasten off on
the wrong side.

French Knot

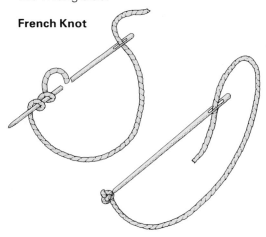

MAKING UP
Once the pieces have been finished refer
to the making up instructions for the
order in which to assemble them.
When joining seams where the pattern
needs to match at any point then the
invisible seam method gives a more
professional finish, but a backstitched
seam is slightly easier and with care can
give just as neat a finish.

Invisible seam
Lay both pieces of fabric to be joined on
a flat surface with the right side facing.
Thread the needle with matching yarn

and join it to the lower edge of one of the
pieces.
Take the needle and insert it into the
center of the first stitch at the lower
edge of the second piece of knitting.

Invisible Seam

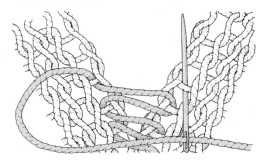

Bring the needle back up through the
stitch above, so picking up the bar
between the rows of stitches.
Pull the yarn through, then take the
needle back across to the first piece of
knitting and repeat. Pull the yarn gently
so that the two pieces of knitting are
drawn together. Insert the needle back
into the second piece of knitting, in the
same place that the needle came out,
and pick up the next bar above, then
repeat again on the first piece of knitting.
Continue in this way to the top of the
seam, gently pulling the yarn every few
stitches to close the seam.
After the last stitch fasten off securely.

Backstitch seam
Place the two pieces to be joined right
sides together.
Thread the needle with matching yarn

Backstitch Seam

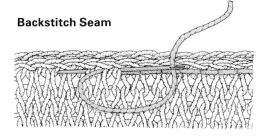

and fasten to the beginning of the seam
with a couple of stitches.
Insert the needle through both

thicknesses and bring it back out again
about ¼"/5mm along the seam. Draw
the needle through, pulling the yarn
gently. Insert the needle back into the
same place that it was inserted the first
time but this time bring it out about
¼"/5mm further along from the last
stitch. Pull the yarn through.
Now insert the needle back into the
fabric at the end of the first stitch and
bring it out again ¼"/5mm further along.
Continue in this way to the end of the
seam, then fasten off securely.

AFTERCARE
After all the hard work of knitting and
making up your garment it is important to
wash it correctly in order to keep it
looking as new.
Always keep a ball band from one of the
balls of yarn that the garment was
knitted with, so that you can always refer
to the washing instructions for that yarn.
If there are no washing instructions on
the ball band, or if you have not kept one,
then hand wash only in cool water. Either
squeeze gently or give a short spin, then
lay the garment flat and ease into shape.
Dry flat away from heat or direct
sunlight.

Acknowledgements
Many thanks to everyone involved in the book, especially Brian:

Debbie Hudson, Sandra Cook, Rose, Winifred Muir, Georgie Eyre, Mavis Thomas, Ron Griffiths and Robert Stell, for their enthusiasm and efficiency in supplying yarn.

Our knitters: Dorothy Herring, Olwyn Webb, Sue Williams, Sue Homeyard, Karl Smith, Naomi, Auntie Dorothy, Rebecca Spencer-Underhill, Elsie Preston, June and Margaret.

Iain McKell and Sue Odell and their studio assistants Dominic Jackson, Charlie Fawell and John Williams.

Vanessa Haines, Ruth Funnell, Vanessa Beiny and Christina Saunders for doing the hair and make-up at the photosessions.

Also Paul Holton, Charlotte, Simon and Matthew.